A Small Band of Brethren

The Beginnings of Churches of Christ in Limestone County, Alabama

John Chisholm Church History Series

C. Wayne Kilpatrick

HERITAGE CHRISTIAN UNIVERSITY PRESS

A Small Band of Brethren: The Beginnings of Churches of Christ in Limestone County, Alabama

Copyright © 2024 by C. Wayne Kilpatrick

Manufactured in the United States

Cataloging-in-Publication Data

Kilpatrick, C. Wayne (Charlie Wayne), 1943–

A Small Band of Brethren: The Beginnings of Churches of Christ in Limestone County, Alabama / by C. Wayne Kilpatrick.

John Chisholm Church History Series

p. cm.

Includes name index.

ISBN: 978-1-956811-77-3 (hdbk); 978-1-956811-78-0 (ebook)

1. Churches of Christ—History—Alabama—Limestone County. 2. Churches of Christ—History—Alabama—Tennessee Valley counties. 3. Churches of Christ—History—Alabama—19th century. I. Author. II. Title. III. Series.

286.676198 DDC20

Library of Congress Control Number: 2024947441

Cover design by Brad McKinnon and Brittany Vander Maas.

Heritage Christian University Press

PO Box HCU
3625 Helton Drive
Florence, Alabama 35630

www.hcu.edu/publications

All rights reserved.

No part of this book may be reproduced in any form or by any electronic or mechanical means, including information storage and retrieval systems, without written permission from the author, except for the use of brief quotations in a book review.

Contents

Foreword	v
Preface	xi
Introduction	xiii
1. Limestone County	1
2. Green Hill—The Stone-Benjamin Lynn Stream	3
3. Mount Pleasant-Campbell Stream of the Limestone County Movement	12
4. Mooresville—Walter Scott and The Evangelist Stream of the Restoration Movement	20
5. Old Reunion	26
6. The Big Creek Group of Churches	43
7. Mount Carmel	60
8. Bethel	73
9. Athens	82
10. Union Grove	95
11. Cartwright	98
12. Oakland	100
13. Holland's Gin	105
14. Corinth	107
Endnotes	110
Bibliography	119
Name Index	121
Also by C. Wayne Kilpatrick	124
Heritage Christian University Press	126

Foreword

Sunday lunch in the home of Kelby and Martha Smith was where the Harps were first impressed upon by Wayne and Brenda Kilpatrick. After four and a half years in the mission field of New Zealand, my young family made its way to Florence, Alabama, in the winter of 1985-86 to attend International Bible College (now Heritage Christian University). Wayne was to be one of my professors. His expertise is in the fields of history and the Bible. That spring semester, it was my privilege to sit in his World History II class. With every passing day, it was apparent that Wayne's passion was all things historical. On the first day, he said, "We must always stop and pay respects to the bridges we have crossed." And, for the next thirteen weeks, he filled the air with the stories of the past. To Wayne, it was not just information on a page that needed to be shared; it was not just the former things that needed retelling. To him, and ultimately to those of us at his feet, it was our past, our story—our history. Whether talking about John Tetzel's sales of indulgences to build Leo X's St. Peter's Cathedral in Rome, Italy, or the rise of Oliver Cromwell's Parliamentarians in the defeat of Charles I of England, we were led through a maze of factual details that resonated and gave more profound meaning to our lives.

Charlie Wayne Kilpatrick was born on Possum Creek, near Center Hill, Lauderdale County, Alabama, on December 30, 1943. He became a Christian under the preaching of Alden Hendrix, being baptized by him in 1957. After two years of undergraduate studies at the University of North Alabama, Wayne was drafted into the U.S. Air Force. Before his international assignment, he took the opportunity to continue his education by taking courses at the University of Maryland. At the height of the Vietnam War, it was not long before he was stationed in England's R.A.F. Welford in Berkshire, where he was assigned the task of ammunition inspector. During his term of service, he attained the level of sergeant. Being a history lover in an old country like England afforded him a goldmine of antiquity to examine firsthand. Whenever leave was extended, he was either playing his banjo somewhere in a show with some of his friends or striking out on his own in a planned direction to investigate Britain's ancient culture.

Returning to the U.S. after his term of service, Wayne was employed for 18 months by the Tennessee Valley Authority. He married the former Brenda Elaine Chaney of Leighton, Alabama, on December 12, 1970. At the encouragement of his brother-in-law, Milton Chaney, a gospel preacher, Wayne entered the first class of International Bible College (now Heritage Christian University) in the spring of 1972. He was part of the college's first class since transitioning from the older Southeastern Institute of the Bible. After graduating with his Bachelor's Degree in Bible in 1974, Wayne determined to return to England as a missionary. Working primarily with the Wembley church of Christ in Middlesex, just northeast of London, he and Brenda evangelized in that region. Due to a lack of sufficient support, after a year, the family returned to the Shoals area.

In the fall of 1975, upon his return to the United States, Wayne accepted an offer to teach World History, Bible Geography, and Church History at International Bible College (now Heritage

Christian University). In addition, he enrolled at Harding University Graduate School of Religion (now Harding School of Theology) to study under noted church historian Earl Irvin West. Wayne completed his studies at Harding with a Master of Arts in Religion (M.A.R.). Over subsequent years, he completed twelve post-graduate hours at the University of Alabama and six graduate hours at the University of North Alabama.

The summer following my first class in World History, it was my pleasure to travel with Wayne Kilpatrick to Newport, Wales, UK, where he directed an evangelistic campaign. For a week in the summer of 1986, we knocked on doors, conducted Bible studies in the city during the day, and worshipped with our Welsh brethren in the evenings. One afternoon, we took a break and went about five miles out of town to Caerleon, an ancient Roman city. We walked through the excavated ruins of the amphitheater and the military barracks. A few days following the campaign, we traveled to London, where we had the pleasure of having our own tour guide, C. Wayne Kilpatrick. Whether at the tower of London, Stonehenge, the cathedrals of Winchester, Canterbury, and Salisbury, and just about everywhere in between, the sheer volume of information that seemed to spill freely from this man's mind was nothing short of phenomenal.

Then, there were Kilpatrick's Church History and Restoration History courses. The names, dates, and stories of the past flowed in graceful order from his lips as if he were walking down memory lane. Wayne had a little yellow box with 4x6 index cards that he used to teach his classes. This coveted container of notes was a veritable treasure trove of knowledge he had collected and shared over the years.

Professor Kilpatrick's classes were a magnet to students. His kind-hearted and sanguine spirit filled every lecture with meaningful material that could be used in our ministry for a lifetime. Once, while teaching the history of the Restoration Movement, we arrived at class, and he told us to go to our cars and follow him a few miles from the school. He took us over to Chisholm Highway to a little shanty of a house. We followed him to the backyard, where among a few trees was the small Chisholm Cemetery. Wayne had just been lecturing about how Benjamin Lynn came to Madison County, Alabama, as early as 1809 to establish New Testament Christianity there. He had explained that Lynn's daughters had married men with that pioneer spirit, Rachel to Marshall De'Spain and Esther to John Chisholm, Jr. Lynn died in 1814 and was buried somewhere north of present-day Huntsville. After 1816, the family moved into what is now Lauderdale County, the Chisholms to Cypress Creek, north of Florence, and the DeSpains to Waterloo.

As we approached the cemetery, there before our eyes were the graves of John and Esther Chisholm. John's father, John Chisholm, Sr., was also buried there. He had been an agent for Cherokee Indian Chief Doublehead and rented land on his reserve. More importantly, these people were the first New Testament Christians in Lauderdale County, planting a New Testament church on Cypress Creek. Also buried in the cemetery was Dorinda Chisholm Hall, the young wife of Benjamin Franklin Hall, the Christian preacher who came to the region in the fall of 1826, preaching baptism for the remission of sins. Under his influence came the baptisms of Tolbert Fanning, Allen Kendrick, and others at the hands of James E. Matthews.

History is a science. With this visit to Chisholm Cemetery, pure science—the ideals, the concepts, the people, the facts on a page—became applied science—seeing, touching, experiencing. Pure history became applied history! It was a hands-on examination of the evidence of history. Later that semester, other trips were made, such as to Red River Meeting House in Logan County, Kentucky, where the Second Great Awakening in America's religious history began under the preaching of Presbyterian James McGready in 1799. We also made our way up to Cane Ridge Meeting House in Bourbon County, Kentucky, where the Kentucky Revival reached a crescendo in August 1801. From there, Wayne took us to Bethany, West Virginia, where we witnessed the artifacts, the home, the buildings of Bethany College, and the old mansion that attests to the lives and influences of Thomas and Alexander Campbell. The lectures, the trips, the discussions, and the demeanor made Wayne Kilpatrick the master of his profession.

C. Wayne Kilpatrick is known for his research and journalism. The sheer volume of hours he has spent in front of microfilm and microfiche readers, computer screens, and books in his hands is uncountable. During one Christmas break many years ago, Wayne read the 40 volumes of Alexander Campbell's *Millennial Harbinger*. He has one of the largest book collections of any historian, above 40,000 volumes. He was a staff writer for *The Alabama Restoration Journal*, and his numerous articles appear in many history-related magazines. He has lectured on church history for many churches of Christ, at numerous universities, and other education-based programs across America.

C. Wayne Kilpatrick is an evangelist and successful gospel preacher. He has conducted semi-annual evangelism campaigns through Heritage Christian University in many of the states of the United States and other countries. For 20+ years, he traveled annually to teach Bible and church history short courses in the Yucatan, Mexico.

After assisting the History Department at Heritage Christian University for 48 years, he received emeritus status in 2022. At the end of this year, he plans to retire from his position to focus on researching and writing on Alabama restoration history.

This tome is a testimony to the tenacity and pure devotion of the man. After reading it, this writer has been impressed by the voluminous sources gleaned to make this work possible. I fully commend C. Wayne Kilpatrick for this book, as it will be most appreciated by researchers of the future when they attempt to dig where he dug. It will be a much-prized resource of Restoration History in North Alabama for generations to come.

Scott Harp
TheRestorationMovement.com
May 17, 2024

Preface

For many years there has been a great need for a comprehensive history of the development of the Restoration Movement in Alabama, and the Tennessee River Valley in general. F. D. Srygley's *Larimore And His Boys* was the earliest attempt to capture any semblance of early Lauderdale County Restoration History, although it was only a partial to the whole of this study. Interest began to manifest itself in the early 1900s. In 1903 A. R. Moore presented a historical review to the Alabama State Board of Missionary Society. This was the first work of its kind, but it was written for the Disciples of Christ—keep in mind that the Disciples were still connected to our movement until 1906. This review was never published. In 1906 J. Waller Henry wrote "Sketches of Pioneer Times" for the *Alabama Christian*—a Disciple paper. Richard L. James and Donald A. Nunnelly wrote graduate theses on the Alabama Restoration Movement. In 1965 George and Mildred Watson published *History of the Christian Churches in the Alabama Area*. All of the above-mentioned material dealt with the Disciples of Christ part of the Restoration Movement. It was not until the 1940s that Asa M. Plyler began traveling over the state and collecting material on the early and then present-day Churches of Christ. He covered every county in the state. His manuscript was finally published upon the request of his family. The book was titled *Historical Sketches of the Churches of Christ in Alabama* and no date of publication was given. Plyler's book gave us some "personally collected information; but beyond that, it has not been of much help, as most of his sources were very limited. Today these sources are more readily available, and we have taken advantage of them.

It was needful—yes even imperative that lives of devotion to the Lord's Kingdom, such as the men and women in this study be told. Younger generations need to know what they have. They need to know that these precious servants of the Lord sacrificed so much so we could be where we are today in the Churches of Christ. A generation, now in danger of squandering away the church, needs to appreciate the fact that many of these subjects went without proper clothing, or proper medical attention many times, were constantly in need of financial means, and made many other sacrifices in order to establish the Lord's work in so many places. It would be the greatest act of ungratefulness toward the generations of these preaching brethren, who gave so much sacrificial devotion to helping save the lost and dying world if their story remains in obscurity. We truly are standing on the shoulders of giants, and these—our predecessors were the giants.

We have undertaken the task of producing a history that uses only documented sources—such as church records, journal articles, unpublished autobiographies, documented papers written for schools and universities, published and unpublished interviews, courthouse records, and even monuments and cemeteries. We have limited this study to the four Alabama counties north of the Tennessee River. That is where the Alabama Restoration Movement began.

This book is written to be used, hopefully, as a resource tool to encourage further research into local church histories. Perhaps, the lives of these forefathers in the Lord's work may inspire us to do great things for our Lord and Savior Jesus Christ.

Introduction

The four counties that lie on the north bank of the Tennessee River—Madison, Jackson, Lauderdale, and Limestone—will be the subject under consideration for this work. We will treat the counties chronologically in the order in which the Restoration Movement began.

At first, Alabama was part of the Mississippi Territory, which was ceded by Georgia and South Carolina to the United States. The Territory of Mississippi was an organized incorporated territory of the United States that existed from April 7, 1798, until December 10, 1817, when the western half of the territory was admitted to the Union as the State of Mississippi and the eastern half became the Alabama Territory until its admittance to the Union as the State of Alabama on December 14, 1819.

Prior to the War of 1812, many settlers came into what is now Madison and Jackson Counties, Alabama. Alabama was then still part of the Mississippi Territory. They could not legally, nor safely travel any further into what is presently known as Northwest Alabama because the Indians controlled the land until 1816. Some of these pioneers settled in northeastern Jackson County near modern day Bridgeport, Alabama. another group settled 10 miles north of Huntsville, Alabama, and established Meridianville.

In the years that followed the close of the War of 1812, an influx of thousands of settlers came into the northern part of Alabama from Tennessee, North and South Carolina, Georgia, and Virginia. This was due to the promise of bounty lands to be given to men who had fought in the War of 1812. With each new settler came his own peculiar religious views, resulting in the founding of churches to propagate their views. Along with these settlers from the older states came the views of Barton Stone, James O'Kelly, and a few years later, Alexander Campbell. Just as with other religious groups, the followers of Stone, O'Kelly, and Campbell founded congregations of believers, who were dedicated to spreading the message of the Restoration Movement. Many of these congregations would prosper for a few years and then gradually disappear. Some, however, would weather the storms of time and exist down to the present.

In Northeast Alabama, the Bridgeport (Rocky Springs) and Meridianville pioneers were neither of the James O'Kelley, Barton Warren Stone nor Alexander Campbell groups. These pioneers began their New Testament churches independent of the other movements. Rocky Springs congregation was established in 1811 or 1812 by members of the Old Philadelphia church in Warren County, Tennessee, which had been established by a people who came from a mixture of religious beliefs and who wanted to follow the New Testament pattern They had established their congregation near Viola, Tennessee in 1808. The Gains and Price families moved shortly afterward to Rocky Springs (1811 or 1812). The Meridianville work was begun by Benjamin Lynn in 1808 or 1809. Both groups had studied themselves out of denominationalism without the influence of any of the three above-mentioned movements.

In Northwest Alabama, one such congregation (Stoney Point —established in 1816) has managed to endure. Several other congregations in this area that were established before the Civil

War, were not so durable. Many of them have faded into obscurity.

Much has been written about the political history of this area, but very little has been written about the religious history. Hardly anything has been written concerning the Restoration Movement in North Alabama. F. D. Srygley's biography of T. B. Larimore, *Larimore and His Boys,* sheds some light upon the history of this area and George and Mildred Watson's *History of the Christian Churches in the Alabama Area* gives some insight into this part of the state. Several histories of local congregations have appeared, but many times these works are weighted down by local traditions, rather than historical facts. Due to the lack of knowledge on the part of the average church member concerning the Restoration Movement, the purpose of this study is to give a historical account of the North Alabama movement. Our method shall be to discover who established these works and what caused them to grow or die, whichever the case may be. Since every historical work must have a beginning and an end, we have set the date of our study to begin with 1808–1809, the approximate time Benjamin Lynn came to Madison County, Alabama, and ending with the year 1914, the year World War I began. This time span covers a little over a hundred years of Alabama restoration history. It should be remembered, however, that this is in no way a complete history because there are examples of churches, such as Liberty, which appeared in *The Christian Register* of 1848 as being in Lauderdale County, Alabama, having eighty-five members, and possessing their own house of worship, then disappearing from all written records. Such incidents make it impossible to compile a complete history. History, however, does not dwell upon that which has been lost, but rather that which can be found. This historical study shall be based upon only what can be found.

To prepare such historical undertaking many sources have been consulted. Local newspapers of the period under discussion, local courthouse records, journals of historical societies, unpublished histories, and biographical sketches have been valuable sources of material. Many books have been written by our brethren on subjects not related to the Alabama area, yet touching upon it, and literature by other religious groups have proven helpful. There are several historical collections of the brotherhood that have supplied valuable aid in this investigation, but the chief source of material has been found in brotherhood journals beginning with Campbell's first issue of *The Christian Baptist* in 1823, through most major journals until the year 2000. Where occasion has demanded and opportunity has afforded, different portions of North Alabama have been visited and much valuable information has been gained by private conversation. Such were the sources from whence this history is derived. It is hoped that this uncovering of information will give a better understanding of the Churches of Christ in North Alabama.

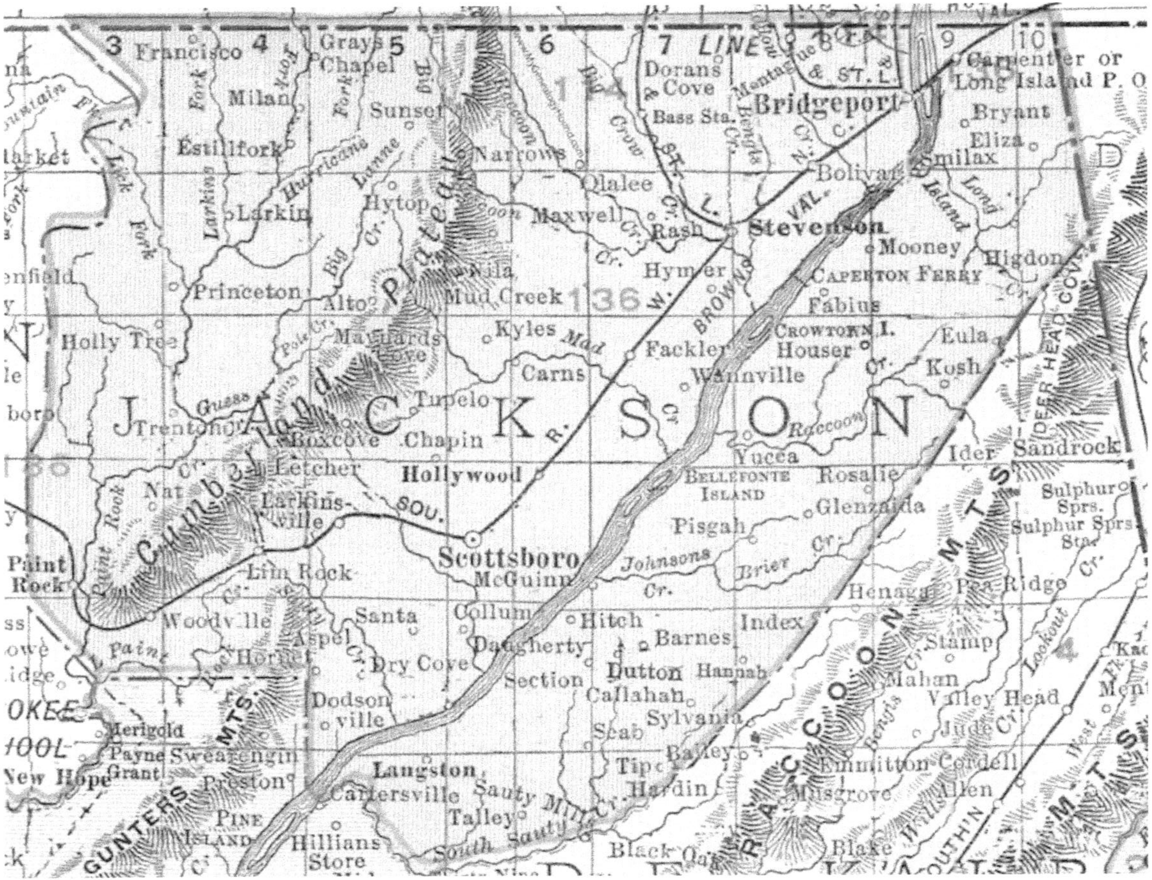
JACKSON
Cumberland Plateau
Scottsboro
Stevenson
Bridgeport
Hollywood
Paint Rock
Francisco
Grays Chapel
Milan
Estillfork
Sunset
Narrows
Larkin
Hytop
Princeton
Alto
Mud Creek
Maxwell
Olalee
Rash
Hymer
Dorans Cove
Bass Sta.
Bolivar
Smilax
Bryant
Eliza
Carpenter or Long Island P. O.
Mooney
Higdon
Caperton Ferry
Fabius
Crowtown I.
Houser
Eula
Kosh
Fackler
Wannville
Kyles
Carns
Tupelo
Chapin
Holly Tree
Trenton
Boxcove
Letcher
Nat
Larkinsville
Lim Rock
Woodville
Santa
Aspel
Hornet
Dry Cove
Dodsonville
Collum
McGuinn
Hitch
Daugherty
Barnes
Dutton
Hannah
Section
Callahan
Sylvania
Seab
Tip
Bailey
Hardin
Langston
Cartersville
Talley
Sauty Mill
South Sauty
Hillians Store
Black Oak
Yucca
Bellefonte Island
Rosalie
Glenzaida
Pisgah
Ider
Sandrock
Sulphur Sprs.
Sulphur Sprs. Sta.
Henagar
Pea Ridge
Index
Stamp
Mahan
Valley Head
Jude
Emmitton
Cordell
Musgrove
Allen
Blake
Merigold
Payne
Grant
Swearengin
Preston
New Hope
Pine Island
Guntersville Mts.
Raccoon Mts.
Lookout Mts.
Deer Head Cove
Raccoon Cr.
Johnsons Cr.
Brier Cr.
Mud Cr.
Paint Rock
Larkins Fork
Lick Fork
Hurricane
Big Cr.
Crow Cr.
Long Island
N. C. & St. L.
W. Brown Val. R.
Sou.
136
7 Line
3
4
5
6
8
9
10

Limestone County

In Asa Monroe Plyler's manuscript from the 1940's he wrote the following introduction in his chapter on Limestone County:

> The section of country that we wish to notice in this chapter is located on the north side of the beautiful Tennessee river, it is west of Madison county and east of Lauderdale county, with the Tennessee line as its boundary on the north. It consists of a little less than four hundred thousand acres, or to be exact 584 square miles. Its population is in all probability more rural than other wise. Athens is its chief city and is the county seat, and a beautiful town indeed it is, with a population of about nine or ten thousand. It has hundreds of nice homes and many fine public buildings.[1]

That was the picture of things in Limestone County, Alabama in the 1940s. Plyler's manuscript was circulated among friends and family for more than sixty years before it was finally published in 2010. The county was organized on February 6, 1818. Limestone County was created by an act of the Alabama Territorial Government. It was taken from the old Mississippi Territorial County of Elk. The new name for the Alabama county was taken from Limestone Creek, which flows through it. The creek bed was of hard Limestone, thus the name. Limestone County consists of fertile agricultural land, scenic hills and waterways that include the Elk River running through the western side, and the Tennessee River on the south.[2]

Limestone County was just a few years behind the other three counties, already discussed in previous chapters, as relates to the Restoration Movement. The first settlers in Limestone County were mostly of Presbyterian, Baptist, and Methodist persuasion religiously—but a fourth group, the Christians, came with these religious pioneers and brought the Restoration Movement. They helped forge religion in Limestone County.

There were three different streams of influence at work in Limestone County within a ten- or twelve-year period—the Stone-Benjamin Lynn stream; the Alexander Campbell stream; and the Walter Scott stream. All three were undeniably present before 1840, as we shall demonstrate within the confines of our Limestone County study. Plyler said according to Adolphus Jackson Rollings that there were only six congregations of the Church of Christ in Limestone County before 1900.[3] That was a sad picture.

Green Hill—The Stone-Benjamin Lynn Stream

First: We must show the Stone-Lynn connection. James Matthews' family was part of the community near Meridianville, Madison County, Alabama. The Lynns, Chisholms, D'Spains, Matthews, and Crisps were all members of the congregation established by Benjamin Lynn around 1809–1810, at Meridianville. Lynn had started his own movement back in Southern Kentucky and then moved to Madison County in 1809. James Matthews became a Christian under the Lynn influence. Lynn's group became affiliated with Barton Warren Stone soon after moving to Alabama. Through the conference-type associations, Matthews and the preachers in Northwest Limestone County were the Stone-Lynn stream. The area around Green Hill became the focal point for that part of the Limestone County Restoration Movement. The first mention of this work came from a very overlooked source—*The Christian Reformer*:

> ... A camp-meeting was holden near Athens, in Limestone County, Alabama, last fall. At this meeting about twenty persons professed faith in Christ, fifteen of whom were baptized. [4]

The meeting near Athens was conducted in the Fall of 1828. It seems likely that James E. Matthews sent the report as his name is mentioned at the beginning of the article in the Christian Reformer. This is the first available reference to the camp meeting site in Limestone County.

Then came the Watson mystery. In George and Mildred Watson's *History of the Christian Churches in the Alabama Area*, they wrote concerning the first established congregation in Limestone County:

> The first Christian Church in this county was organized in 1829 by Elders Green and Hill (possibly Green Hill) about five miles northwest of Athens. This church was perpetuated as Green Hill Camp Ground until 1848. When this mother church declined, others arose out of it. Among notable members were the parents of Andrew Witty, Brother Weatherford, and David Eckerberger of Athens.[5]

We are in a quandary about this information. First, we can find no evidence that there were elders named Green and Hill attending this meeting. From where did this information come? The date sounds credible, but where is it documented? James Evans Matthews, who was present for at least the first few camp meetings at this place, mentions nothing of these two elders (preachers in the 1820s and 30s). There was, however, a preacher by the name of Abner Hill, who lived near Tuscumbia at this time. There were also two men by the name of Green listed among the Tennessee-Alabama preachers—John Green of Lebanon, Tennessee, and James Y. Green of Hurts Cross Roads, Tennessee. All three men were members of the Christian Conference of North Alabama-South Middle Tennessee. These three men were never listed among the preachers who attended these camp meetings near Athens. The rest of the Watson information checks with the facts. The more probable explanation for the name was the site of the camp meetings was covered with green hills. This writer has visited the old campsite and that is what he saw—"green hills" and a valley with a clear stream of water coursing its way to the Elk River. If the Watsons have discovered a tidbit of information to be true, that no one else has seen—what happened to it? J. Waller Henry wrote several sketches of the early Alabama movement, with as many errors as facts. These sketches were published in the *Alabama Christian* from February 1906 through July 1906. Several of these sketches are missing. It could be that he was the source for the Watson's comment about how Green Hill was named and established. If their information is correct, it may be that Green Hill was the oldest congregation in the Limestone County Restoration Movement. That would have been five years before J. K. Speer's report of a congregation in Limestone County.

How did Green Hill become so prominent in the North Alabama movement? Andrew Ellis, a historian of Limestone County Churches of Christ also wrote of the Green Hill meeting place. In a footnote, he wrote the following:

> Christian Messenger, Barton W. Stone, Editions from September 24, 1827; November 30, 1830, 1831, James Matthews reported and supported the Christian Messenger until around 1848 and for a period of nearly 20 years from 1829-1848 Matthews mentioned the gatherings and camp meetings in Athens, Ala. Green Hill campground, Witty Mill Creek still stands, however no current remnants are there from the era mentioned above.[6]

So, Ellis gave a name for the creek that ran through the campground. Ellis was apparently unaware that W.S. Speer, J. H. Dunn, and James Ragin Collinsworth all reported on meetings at the Green Hill Church between 1845 through 1848 because he never alluded to them. This will be discussed on another page.

We now begin an examination of Matthews' letters. He was, as Jack Lewis said—"a who done it" and not "a me too-er." In other words, he was a participant in these early beginnings across the Northernmost counties of Alabama. The following is an extract of a letter from Elder James E. Matthews. Lauderdale County, (Ala.) Sept. 24, 1827:

> Dear Brother — I have just returned from a tour of three weeks, during which time I attended three Camp Meetings: One in Limestone County, one in Morgan, and one in Blount. In Limestone we had a reviving time. About 20 joined the church— 15 were baptized, and several others believed. Among those who were baptized was David R. Scott and his Lady, who formerly resided near you. They wish this intelligence communicated to their friends. When we take into view the infantile state of the Church in the above County, it is lacking popularity, and the violent opposition of our popular brethren, we may safely say that the progress of truth was beyond what we had anticipated. — And what renders this revival still more gratifying, is, that it does not consist merely in speculation; for the people appeared to enjoy that heavenly-minded disposition, which makes them of one mind and one soul.[7]

When we view the infantile state of the church in the above county, it is lacking popularity, and the violent opposition of our popular brethren, we may safely say that the progress of truth was beyond what we had anticipated. — And what renders this revival still more gratifying, is, that it does not consist merely in speculation; for the people appeared to enjoy that heavenly-minded disposition, which makes them of one mind and one soul.[8]

The same was so with Limestone—thus Green Hill campground was the designated site for Limestone County. There was plenty of grass and water for the animals and a pleasant valley that gave the feel of a safe harbor for the meetings and conferences that were held there. The congregation that met there was an established church, known as the Green Hill Church of Christ.[9]

Matthews wrote a second report including Limestone

County, along with other North Alabama and South Middle Tennessee counties. The following is a short extract from that letter dated: Lauderdale County, Ala. Nov. 30, 1828: "I have been informed that at a Camp Meeting, near Athens, in Limestone County, about 20 professed faith in Christ, 15 of whom were baptized."[10]

Matthews sent another report in October, and it was published in December 1829. He wrote:

> Elder Jas. E. Matthews, of Lauderdale, Ala. writes, Oct. 9— Our Camp-meeting (At Republican near Florence) terminated about 10 days ago. As I had expected, we had a glorious time.... The next week at Conference in Limestone County, Ala., about 40 professed, 18 of whom were baptized To conclude, The Lord has done great things for us, whereof we are glad, and I verily believe that the latter day of glory is at hand. Yours in the bonds of the gospel.[11]

In another extract from Elder J. E. Matthews, Barton's Ala., dated October 29, 1830, he wrote:

> I hasten to give you some information respecting the progress of religion in this country lately. At the Camp Meeting in McNairy county Tenn. near M. W. Matthews, held on the 3d Lord's day in Sept. 22 were immersed. At Purdy in the same co. the week following, about 10 were united with the church. At Republican, the week following 26 were immersed, and several belonging to other churches united with us in a church relationship. The Sunday following, I baptized 4 at my house. The next week a Camp Meeting was held both in Limestone county and in Morgan. In Limestone I am informed that about 25 united with the church. In Morgan 7. We have experienced great opposition at the last place, but I think that truth gained ground rapidly at the late meeting there.[12]

One can see the steady progress of the Green Hill area of the county. The next report we give in full:

> Bartons, Ala. Dec. 12, 1831: Dear Brother: Our Conference commenced on the last day of Sept. During the meeting 19 persons were immersed, and a number more professed faith in Jesus: most of whom have been baptized since. In Limestone county 23 were immersed, and others confessed the Lord Jesus. In Morgan Co. 4 were immersed; and in Blount county 8 were baptized, and several from other societies united with us.
>
> At all the camp-meetings in North Alabama, and in the South of Tennessee, about 176 persons put on the Christian name by immersion, and from the best information that I have received probably 180 more have been added to the churches since.
>
> The following Elders were present at Conference, viz. John Mulkey, Isaac Mulkey, John Hooton, William Hooton, John M'Donald, Elisha Randolph, Eph. D. Moore, James Anderson, Tolbert Fannin, Mansel W. Matthews, and me.
>
> In Conference, we dispensed with the etiquette usually observed. No bishop was called to the chair, nor was any clergyman or lay-member chosen President. We entered no resolves upon our minute book, nor did we take the name of an "Advisory Council." But "with one accord, in one place" we mutually engaged in arranging the appointments for our next annual meetings, so as to best promote the cause of the Redeemer; and agreed to request you to publish said appointments in the Christian Messenger. Jas. E. Matthews.
>
> Camp meeting appointments deferred for next No.[13]

When the next series of meetings were announced the Limestone County appointment was "1st Lord's day in August" 1832. [14] The reason the camp meetings' importance was declining is explained by James E. Matthews in an extract:

Extract from Elder Jas. E. Matthews. Barton's, Lauderdale Co, Alabama. Oct 24, 1832: ...I have long been the advocate of reformation, but I view with extreme regret the spirit which to me seems to prevail among many of those who profess to be reformers. We should certainly proclaim the truth fearlessly. but we should avoid that precipitancy which I fear too much prevails in adopting a new idea. Teachers of the religion of Jesus, should feel so solemnly the responsibility resting upon them, as not lightly to proclaim as truth that which is questionable. But this is probably not the greatest evil that is obtaining among us, especially our young brethren. It appears to me that there is too much rashness and self-confidence with a censorious spirit manifested in their discourses, for them to be profitable. They seem to justify themselves by the plea that they are teaching the truth, not remembering, I fear, that they should "Speak the truth in love..."[15]

The final list of annual meetings that related to Alabama was published in September 1833. It simply stated that "3d. Lord's day, in August Limestone County, Alabama."[16] Matthews had written a comment on the status of the meetings in Alabama. This especially impacted the Green Hill work:

Bro Jas. E. Matthews, of Ala. writes, Aug. 8, That at their late annual meeting, 8 persons were added to the church by immersion— that large accessions have taken place in Tennessee in many places— that the churches in Alabama are gradually increasing, and the prospects brightening. The preaching brethren are becoming alive to the work.[17]

The next meeting, that we learn about was ten years later and never reported in the journals. It took place in 1843 and Allen Kendrick conducted it. He baptized Sister Mary A., wife of A. J. Weatherford during the meeting. It was only by the obituary that we ever heard of the 1843 meeting. S. F. McGlocklin wrote sister

Weatherford's obituary. His statement on Green Hill was simply: "She lived a devoted Christian life for fifty years, as she was baptized by Brother Allen Kendrick, at old Green Hill campground, in the year 1843."[18]

Tolbert Fanning gave a summary of J. R. Collinsworth's meeting in October 1844:

> Brother James Collinsworth, of Athens, Ala., held a meeting at Green Hill, five miles from that place, in the month of Oct., at which fourteen were added to the faithful. Brother C.'s letter would have been given in full had I been at home in November. T. F.[19]

Collinsworth made his home at Green Hill for a few years. As is evident in the next report. It was sent in by W. S. Speer (son of Joshua K. Speer):

> I held a protracted camp meeting at Green Hill, Limestone Co. Alabama, from the 3d to the 8th inst., inclusive. I preached sixteen times. No other preacher participated, except our excellent brother. J. Collingsworth, who, being at home, literally refused to speak. We had rain and mud in abundance. The meeting closed with thirty-two additions. Prospects happy— Farewell. W. S. Speer. October 11, 1845.[20]

Meetings, to a lesser extent, continued at Green Hill for a few more years. In 1845 W. S. Speer reported on one such meeting: He mentioned the fact that it was a protracted meeting. It was not on the scale of the annual camp meetings. He also mentioned that J. Collinsworth (James Ragin Collinsworth) was the located minister. The number of additions was impressive. Two years later Collinsworth wrote an inquiry to S, B. Aden of the *Christian Messenger* and *Bible Advocate*. His address was still Limestone County.[21]

In 1848 John Henry Dunn sent a call for a co-operation

meeting for North Alabama churches. It also was published in the *Christian Messenger* and *Bible Advocate*:

> A co-operation meeting of the Churches in North Alabama will commence on Friday before the third Lord's day, in October next, at Green Hill meeting house, seven miles north of Athens, Limestone county, Alabama. We respectfully solicit the aid of preaching brethren from Tennessee and elsewhere. Ample provisions are being made to entertain all who may come. Many of the brethren speak of camping on the ground.[22] Dunn mentioned that the meeting would take place "at Green Hill meeting house, seven miles north of Athens," [22]

There was obviously a viable congregation at Green Hill as late as 1848. Just scraps and pieces are all that we can find on the church at Green Hill, since then. This still reveals just how important Green Hill was to the Limestone County work. Maybe some historians of the future will find more information on Green Hill.

Mount Pleasant-Campbell Stream of the Limestone County Movement

How did the Campbell influence make its way into Limestone County when nearly all the North Alabama churches favored Barton Stone's movement? That will be answered in this section on the Poplar Creek-Mount Pleasant work. To begin answering this question we must travel up into South Middle Tennessee. In *A Baptist History of Middle Tennessee*, we read:

> Alexander Campbell came upon the stage of action and soon (in a way) connected himself with the Baptists. He at once began his campaign of Arminianism among the Baptists and soon poisoned the minds of many in their ranks. Even where he did not go himself his publications and converts did, till the whole Baptist brotherhood of this country was stirred, some in advocacy of his views, others in opposition to them. Soon those who fell in with his views began an opposition to the doctrines of the Baptists. They first began a fight against the "doctrine of limited atonement," and declared that Christ died for all mankind, "for every individual of the human race, for Pharaoh and Judas as much as for Abraham and Paul." (Bond's History of Concord Association, page 38.) They also stated that the doctrine held by the Baptists of "personal, particular and unconditional election

was the doctrine of men and devils." (*History of Concord Association*, page 39.) Thus the war went on, none ever dreaming of the purpose of A. Campbell.[23]

A rift had come among the Baptist churches in Middle Tennessee. At the time of the organization, this Association (Concord) covered all the territory in this division of the State between Nashville and the Cumberland range of mountains.

The following explains how the rift began:

> Finally, in 1826, this sentiment had grown in Elk River Association (which covered the territory embraced by the counties lying in the southern part of Middle Tennessee and reaching as far north as Rutherford County), till it resulted in a division led by Elder Wm. Keele. Elder Keele was a member of Liberty Church in Rutherford County, and the first breach spoken of by his biographer is in these words: "The disagreement between the two parties was first made public at a meeting at Liberty Church in Rutherford County. The Rev. William Keele was sitting in the old-fashioned stand, which was found in all the houses of worship in those days; and when he saw that the difficulty was not likely to be adjusted with honor to the free grace (Arminian) party, he leaped over the top of the stand, and rushed from the house, calling all to follow who believed as he did. Thereupon a great rushing was made from the house, until by far the greater part of the congregation was rapidly following the Rev. William Keele. He preached to them under the shade of some trees that stood near and made other appointments for the future. This was the origin of the Separate Baptist Church." (*Life of Rev. William Keele*, pages 54–55). This was the first formal action toward the formation of what is now known as Separate Baptists in Middle Tennessee. This was most probably in the spring of 1826 and was the signal for action with other churches. By the meeting of Elk River Association in 1826, things were ripe for action and a formal division was the result, the following on

either side being very nearly equal in strength. The party withdrawing, led by the said Elder William Keele, formed the Duck River Association of Separate Baptists.[24]

By this time, the majority of Baptists in this part of Tennessee had become Separate Baptists and many became a part of our Restoration Movement. From 1827 until 1836 the Baptist lost 42 preachers to the Restoration Movement.[25] The Flint River Association became a feeder association to the Duck River Association. John Favor was originally an active member of the Flint River Association. Hosea Holcombe said the following of John Favor:

> Mr. John Favor was ordained in 1822 and was dismissed the next year. It is believed that in consequence of some unhappy circumstances, which occurred in some of the churches, Mr. Favor was led to join the separate Baptists about Duck River, in Tennessee. There was a number who followed him; at length he became a Campbellite and is now dead. Mr. Favor was believed to be a good man.[26]

Men like Wade Barrett of Giles County, Tennessee; Willis Hopwood of Marshall County, Tennessee; Joshua Kennerly Speer of Rutherford County, Tennessee, all became reformers. John Favor was a friend of Joshua K. Speer as we shall see later. He was probably friends with the rest of these men, and they were all becoming connected to Alexander Campbell's movement. This is how Campbell's influence made its way into Limestone County, Alabama.

When John Favor came into Limestone County, he bought land almost immediately. His first purchase was on April 7, 1818. He purchased the Northeast ¼ of section 34, township 3, Range 5 West, certificate number 277.[27] In 1823 Favor gave two acres to the Round Island Baptist Church to build a house of worship.[28] Bobby Graham wrote from information in a *History of Round*

Island Baptist Church by Dave Hurst a pharmacist in Athens, as follows:

> Dave Hurst, a Registered Pharmacist in Athens, Alabama, and then a member of Round Island, wrote a history of Round Island Baptist Church, which he called "Remember and Rejoice, 1817–1992" (6–7). In his mention of the years of Favor's problems at Round Island, he says that six of the original members asked for and received letters of dismission from Round Island in August 1822. In October those six and several others who had joined Round Island after its formation, left to form Poplar Creek Baptist Church of Christ. This new congregation became the mother church of another group formed in 1827—Independent Poplar Creek Baptist Church of Christ. Favor's son, John Favor, Jr. was selected to be the pastor of this church. Favor, Jr. had been ordained at Elim (original name of the Athens First Baptist Church). Hurst says that there had been problems with the Favor family at Round Island for about two years. The minutes indicate that both father and son had disrupted services and business meetings and had accused the pastor of teaching the "abominable doctrines of the Church at Rome." Round Island made formal charges against the Favors and later demanded that the new church at Poplar Creek judge and discipline them. When Poplar Creek refused Round Island's demand, there followed a period of peace. The matter must have grown serious, because the Flint River Association had a committee investigate it in 1826, and to mediate peace between the two churches. Minutes from 1827 reveal that the association broke fellowship with the two men because they were adamant and unrepentant. Hurst adds, "All this from the family who had donated the land upon which the church was built!" He also opines that the Favors had disagreed with the manner in which the Round Island Church had dealt with some who were not living up to standards set by the Rules of Decorum.[29]

As early as March 1828, Favor was an agent for Campbell's *Christian Baptist*;[30] to which many of the Separate Baptists of Tennessee subscribed. His trouble between Round Island and Poplar Creek had driven him further away from the United Baptist and now Campbell's material just hardened the relationship. He continued as an agent until Campbell discontinued the *Christian Baptist* in July 1830. In July 1829 Favor sent in a subscription for J. N. Biard[31] (connected to Stone's family) at Ripley, Limestone County; and in December he sent for his good friend Joshua Speer, J. M. Dement, a member at Poplar Creek, and J. N. Smith.[32] To finalize his relationship with Round Island he joined the Duck River Association of Middle Tennessee. By September 4, 1829, John Favor, John Nelson Biard, and Thomas Dement were messengers from Poplar Creek to the Duck River Association, meeting at Flat Creek, Bedford County, Tennessee.[33] This is where Favor was getting serious about reformation. The first true sign of a transition from Baptists to the reformers was printed in Alexander Campbell's *Millennial Harbinger*. It came through a report by Joshua K. Speer:

> Cannon's Creek, Maury county, Ten., December 4, 1833. I attended a four-day meeting (including the 4th Lord's day in October last) at Poplar Creek, Limestone county, Alabama; where I had the pleasure of declaring "the glad tidings concerning the kingdom of God and the name of Jesus Christ," for two hours on each day, to an attentive audience. Eight persons confessed that Jesus Christ is Lord by submitting to the institution of immersion for the remission of sins. We had, truly, a time of refreshing from the presence of the Lord. The reformation has made a very fair beginning in Limestone county, having amongst its advocates several of the more intelligent part of the community, a number of whom have shared largely in the honors of this world, but are now willing to seek "the honor which comes from God only." Joshua K. Speer.[34]

Speer was one of the many Baptist preachers who left the Baptist Church in Middle Tennessee. He was a close friend of the Favors. This may very well have been the first time the people, at that place, ever heard the gospel preached by anyone except the Favors.

John Favor, Sr., sent a report to Walter Scott's *Evangelist*. He reported the following:

> We separated from the Baptists a few years ago on account of some difference on church government; we then took the appellation of 'Independent Baptists,' we were twelve in number; we have since determined to take the living oracles for our guide in both faith and practice; we meet on every first day of the week to break bread, we have a Bishop who labors in word and doctrine, also three Elders who preside in the church, and Deacons. Our number is above one hundred at this time: we have frequent additions by confession and immersion. Yours in gospel bonds. John Tarver (Favor), Sen. Limestone, Alabama.[35]

In this report, he told how the church was organized. He also gave the reason they disputed with the Baptist church. It was over church government and doctrine. Scott corrected the misspelling of Favor's name in a short statement later:

Brother John Faver (Favor), Senior, writes, that in Athens, Alabama, they have a church of 100 members.[36]

John Favor, Jr., the minister of the newly formed Mt. Pleasant church near Poplar Creek, sent the next report to Campbell. It was ten months later but still reflected on Speer's meeting the previous year. Favor, Jr. wrote:

> Athens, Limestone county, Ala. October 16, 1834. The good cause is progressing in my neighborhood. Between 60 and 70 have made the good confession, and were immersed for remission, since the meeting of which brother Speer informed you, or within 12 months past. These have all been added to the congre-

gation at Mount Pleasant, near Poplar Creek. The disciples, with a few exceptions, are growing in grace and in the knowledge of our Lord Jesus Christ.

We have been meeting for worship on the first day of the week for more than two years and can confidently say that the doctrine is of God. At a 3 days' meeting, held at Mount Pleasant, including last Lord's day, attended by brethren Anderson and Griffin, 10 confessed the Lord and were added to the congregation. The opposition is raging; but the truth is mighty and will prevail. John Favor, Jun.[37]

Since Speer's meeting the year before, the Favors abandoned the Poplar Creek name and established the Mt. Pleasant church. From 60 to 70 persons had put on Christ through baptism for the remission of sins within the last year. Favor gives a clue as to when the group became a New Testament church. He said: "We have been meeting for worship on the first day of the week for more than two years and can confidently say that the doctrine is of God." We learn that James Clark Anderson from Rocky Springs Congregation in Jackson County, Alabama, and his preaching partner Thacker V. Griffith who grew up near Meridianville, Alabama held a three-day meeting at Mt. Pleasant. So, now the Mt. Pleasant congregation was being exposed to other reformers.

John Favor, Sr., died before 1838, according to DAR records.[38] The congregation continued for several years after John, Sr. died. It was still around for a short period after the Civil War. One event occurred in September 1869:

An interesting meeting which has been in progress for some time at Poplar Creek was brought to a close on Sunday night. The services were conducted by Elder J. H. Dunn of the Christian Church, and six persons connected themselves with the church.[39]

This is the last thing that we could document on the work of the Favors and the Mt. Pleasant/Poplar Creek connection. From this study one can clearly see the Campbell connection through John Favor, Sr., and how it impacted the Limestone County movement.

As a side note to one of Favor's co-workers (John Nelson Biard), we take a short look at the Biard-Stone family's history. John Stone was the father of Ezekiel and Barton Warren Stone. Ezekiel Stone was the father of Rebecca Stone, who married John Nelson Biard. Barton W. Stone later came to Limestone County and visited the Biard family. It is recorded:

> During the years in North Alabama in the old Cherokee Nation the settlement has an eight-sided log cabin on the Tennessee River, and here Barton W. preached ... Stone was an accomplished linguist, preached to the Cherokee in their own language. Some of those sermons he preached are still in the Biard family.[40]

Mooresville— Walter Scott and The Evangelist Stream of the Restoration Movement

Mooresville is a beautiful village that sits on the Tennessee River in southeast Limestone County, Alabama. It was incorporated on November 16, 1818. It is the oldest town in Limestone County. Tradition says the first settler was William Moore. Today, visitors to historic Mooresville find beautiful, well-maintained, antebellum homes. When one enters this small village, it is as though he has taken a step back a hundred years in time. The people of Mooresville pride themselves in preserving the village, intact, for posterity.

It was in this beautiful village that J. H. Hundley began reading the writings in Walter Scott's journal, *The Evangelist*. By August 1839, he was convinced that he should be "immersed for the remission of sins."[41] He wrote a letter to the brethren in Tuscumbia, requesting that they send someone to Mooresville to immerse him. They sent Carroll Kendrick[42] who preached several sermons there and by May 1, 1840, had helped the Mooresville congregation to form and grow to seventy in number. The work continued to thrive at Mooresville until 1844 when the followers of Dr. John Thomas began to take their toll upon the small band. The Thomasites were sometimes called the "New Revelation Sect."[43] Tolbert Fanning stopped at Mooresville on September 19, 1844, and preached to the brethren.[44] In 1845 G. W. Elley and J. H. Morton came and held a meeting, during which one of Mooresville's strongest future Christians was baptized—Martha Ann Tisdale Peebles. It was said of her that few men or women ever tried to acquire such a devotion and zeal for the holy principles, as she did.[45] Up until 1846, the Mooresville church had been meeting in a "free house of worship," a building built for all religious groups to use. Sometime in the early spring, the Presbyterians had shut our brethren from the building.[46] By this time the church was in a deplorable condition at Mooresville. One reason the church was in a sad condition was the fact that there was no regular minister at Mooresville. By 1849, J. H. Dunn had moved into the county, near Athens, and was now frequenting the Mooresville brethren with preaching visits.[47] He tried to solicit a preacher who could teach in the community school, the idea being that the preacher could support himself while he preached at Mooresville since the brethren could not support him. Fanning tried to make the situation look appealing by pointing out that the school patronage and aid of the churches would doubtlessly give "handsome support."[48]

For the next two years, the brethren struggled along without the aid of a full-time preacher, depending solely upon Brother Dunn's visits and a frequent visit from some brother passing through. One such visit came when J. J. Trott stopped and preached at Mooresville in May of 1851. He wrote concerning the work in that place:

> They have a very good brother for an overseer but have suffered much for want of 'regular preaching.' We could not stay long enough to do much good. Nothing less than two or three continued efforts, in my judgment, can bring about a reaction for the better.[49]

Another reason the brethren were suffering was because they had no regular place in which to meet, except the member's home. They were in the process of raising funds for a meeting house to be shared with the Sons of Temperance. Later that year on December 14, 1851, Trott stopped, while on his way back to Nashville. He fully intended to preach several times, but, after one sermon, he returned to Nashville because of wintry weather.[50] In the months of November and December of 1852, J. H. Dunn baptized nine persons at Mooresville.[51]

For the next two years, growth was slow but Dunn kept encouraging the brethren in their work for God's kingdom. They managed to build a building by 1854. The land had been purchased on October 29, 1851, for a sum of $20.00 from James Clement.[52] They shared their meeting house with the Odd Fellows and Sons of Temperance. November 22, 23, and 24, 1856, J. H. Dunn preached three days, Saturday, Sunday, and Monday to the Mooresville church. One was restored and six were immersed.[53] He was joined in this effort by Crockett McDonald of Moulton. In the last week of May 1857, he held a three-day meeting, and four more were added to the Mooresville church. At this point, several members of the Presbyterian Church had united with the brethren. No wonder the Presbyterian minister said that the "church of Christ down on the corner was hatched out in the mud sills of Hell, and from an egg laid by the Devil."[54] On Thursday, November 26, 1857, Tolbert Fanning came and preached four sermons and left the following day. One person was baptized at this time.[55]

While Fanning was at Mooresville, he had to deal with an unpleasant situation. The brethren felt that they could not worship God unless the service was conducted by "officers."[56] The brethren finally agreed to attend their worship as "Christians," and to dispense with "official service." The leading figure at Mooresville was J. H. Hundley, its first charter member, and the man responsible for the establishing of the work at this place. It was upon his insistence that Carroll Kendrick came to baptize him. His baptism made him the first Christian in Mooresville. Brother Hundley authored a book, *The Plan of Salvation*, in 1858.[57] The book contained eighty-eight pages and was acclaimed to be one of the best on the subject. It was Hundley who had guided the congregation thus far. One is only left to guess what the source of trouble at this congregation was; but, despite Fanning's teachings on the subject and Hundley's leadership, the old problem was at work again.

In July of 1860, O. P. Miller of Washington, D. C. had come to hold a meeting. At the very outset of the meeting, trouble arose. Miller, being a mature-minded gospel preacher, dealt with the problem and continued his meeting for ten days. Ten souls were added to the church, some of whom were "the influential of the community." The meetings, according to Miller, were well attended and the whole community seemed "ready to hear the truth."[58] Shortly after this meeting, the devil was at work at Mooresville once more. The old "official worship" question came about again. On October 2, 1860, Fanning came back and confronted the problem again. The older members seemed inclined to believe the need for "officials" in the service. Fanning said most of his time was spent restoring peace.[59] Fanning did baptize a "Baptist friend" who wanted to be baptized for remission of sins, while at this place. The year 1860 had been one of the better years for Mooresville.

The year 1861 brought sorrow in two ways. The Civil War would come to this area and one of the younger members, Johnny Tucker died in the prime of life. He was nearly twenty-three and had been a Christian for four years.[60] It was in the younger men like him, that the hope of the future Mooresville church lay. The war brought much hardship upon this area around Mooresville. Union soldiers camped near here and often made forages into the village, seeking food, horsed, and anything else they could take. During the Union encampment, James A. Garfield, a Union colonel, and gospel preacher was invited to come preach to the Mooresville brethren. In a letter to his wife, he wrote:

> There is a church in the village of Mooresville nearby and they have sent up inviting me to speak to them on Sunday. If I am not too unwell, I have a notion to speak to them.[61]

Apparently, he was well enough to speak. The brethren of Mooresville boast, even today, of him having spoken in their building. One can even look upon the Bible, said to have been used by Garfield.

After the war, J. M. Pickens came to North Alabama to work. In September of that year, he called for a consultation meeting at Mooresville.[62] He found a handful of war-weary Christians. they had lost most of their money, food sources, and other things that make life livable. The congregation had gone into the war with twenty-five members, even after the good year of 1860, in which they increased in number. It was these sad conditions that prompted J. M. Pickens to write: "There is great destitution and want among many of the people of North Alabama."[63]

Mooresville was truly in destitution, both spiritually and physically. For five years, silence seemed to fall upon the work in this place and no reports were made during this period concerning the work there.

Finally, the silence was broken on April 17, 1872, by a brother W. G. Martin in a letter to David Lipscomb. The question of a woman leaving her husband over mistreatment had arisen at Mooresville. Lipscomb promptly pointed the brother to Matthew chapter 19. For nearly two more years silence once again fell over the work in this place. Then in the last week of June 1877, T. B. Larimore held a meeting at Mooresville, resulting in eleven additions to the church. He paid the small band a very high compliment in writing:

> When they invite a teaching brother to visit them, the understanding is not that he is to labor 'for' them, but 'with' them. They work while he works and sometimes, they work while he sleeps.[64]

In the first week of July 1880, E. A. Elam, who had just graduated from Burritt College a year before, came and held a four-day meeting with three additions.[65] After Elam's meeting, nothing further was written concerning Mooresville until October 27, 1888, when A. R. Moore reported that he was to hold a meeting at Mooresville but was prevented from holding it due to a yellow fever epidemic, six miles away at Decatur.[66]

Mooresville had reached its peak and was now left to struggle for survival. The future did not look very bright. By 1906 a total of 722 Christians were to be found in Limestone County, Alabama.[67] Of all the Christians found in Limestone County, only a handful were located in Mooresville.

Looking back, one wonders how the work at Mooresville endured since they have never had a full-time preacher. Their problems over "official service" and the taint of the "New Revelations" sect hindered their growth at times when other churches were growing. The opposition from their Presbyterian neighbors never was a major problem but did cause some concern at times. They did manage to survive, however, even when other surrounding churches were dying during the Civil War. With the determination to survive without permanent preaching, one is left to wonder how the work would have grown with a full-time preacher.

From 1906 until its closing in 1997—the congregation was small but dedicated. Their later years brought dependence upon other congregations for help. Their help came from the surrounding churches in recent years. The brethren at Beltline in Decatur helped considerably in the last few years.

Today the building stands as a silent sentinel to the past and is a beacon for the future. Except for special occasions, the old church house is unused. It made a permanent mark on the surrounding area and especially on Limestone County.

Old Reunion

The second congregation in the eastern portion of Limestone County was Reunion—later called "Old Reunion." J. H. Hundley had a large part in establishing Reunion, as he owned a large plantation near the location of Reunion. From a paper prepared by A. J. Rollings:

> An old settler of the community says his father and uncle helped to build the meeting house and the deed is dated 1858. The old building still stands and is used.[68]

Possibly the first hint of the area around Reunion was a vague reference by Tolbert Fanning to J. H. Hundley's home in the *Christian Review* of 1844:

> On the 19th, I visited Mooresville, in Limestone county, and addressed quite an attentive congregation at night, and on Wednesday morning. Few of the good people in this section are as willing to trust the great truth recorded in the Bible as they are the "new revelations" for which they pray at camp meetings. Our venerable Bro. Hunley, a few miles distant, I am persuaded will exert a happy influence on the surrounding country.[69]

By this report, we learn that Hundley was no longer living in Mooresville. He did not move to Huntsville until after the Civil War, therefore Hundley's home must have been near Reunion, as he owned property in that place. During the time of Fanning's visit, the congregation was still in the formative stage—house church phase.

The first report from the *Gospel Advocate* on Reunion is from Tolbert Fanning:

> We spent from Sept. 29th to October 7th in Limestone county, Ala., and we feel assured that our labor, though in some respects unsatisfactory to ourselves, was not in vain.
>
> At Re-Union, seven miles from Athens, we met, on Lord's day the 30th of September, brethren John H. Dunn, Wade Barrett, and John H. Hundly. All were far advanced in life, and, to our mind, very much devoted to the cause of our Master. We preached on Lord's day and Monday, and during our stay, there were some eighteen additions reported. We left brethren Dunn and Barrett to continue the meeting, and from all the prospects, we doubt not more additions were made to the Lord. We were much rejoiced on Monday at the adjustment of difficulties between even seniors of the congregation who had been much alienated from each other. We trust the beloved brethren will take warning.[70]

After Fanning returned to Nashville J. H. Dunn wrote a follow-up report:

> Brother Fanning: After you left Reunion, brother Barrett and I continued the meeting to Tuesday afternoon I and succeeded in persuading some others to become obedient to our Lord, several were heads of families. There were twenty additions in all; twelve confessions, and eight more who had been members. The disciples were much revived, built up, strengthened, and greatly encouraged. There were no efforts made at eloquence

and rhetoric, but a calm and solemn exhibition of truth, which reached the heart of many who were in attendance. The triumph was achieved by the eloquence of facts. Your brother in the one hope, J. H. Dunn, Lone Mulberry, Ala, Oct. 4, 1860.[71]

This would be the last report on Reunion until after the Civil War, J. H. Dunn helped keep the work at Reunion during the war. He rode as far as Stoney Point assisting the churches and keeping them alive. John Taylor was also doing the same in the northwestern corner of Alabama. The war ended in 1865, but it took a couple of years before newspapers and journals were fully in production. J. H. Dunn sent the first report on Reunion in 1867. The report read as follows:

> On last Saturday, I went to Reunion, for the purpose of aiding the brethren, in settling a difficulty in the congregation.
> I met our beloved brother Smith of Tennessee, who left us after preaching.
> On the Lord's day. I continued the meeting up to last night, preaching of nights only. The results of our effort was six additions, three from the world; one from the Methodists, one from the Baptists, and one took membership who had belonged to a congregation of disciples in the State of Illinois. Add to the above numbers two additions made to the congregation at Reunion in July, one of whom was from the Baptists, and the other had belonged to a congregation which is extinct, and we have eighteen additions since the middle of July. There was no undue excitement at the above-named meetings; all was affected by the simple truth, and arguments based upon admitted principles. The denominations in this section are making a tremendous effort at this time. Pilate and Herod has made friends, for the time being, and while this friendship or union lasts, (for it is temporary) that thing called Campbellism suffers severe castigations. I never saw the people of this country more anxious to hear the truth, than at this time. Sensible and thinking people

seem determined not to be entrammeled by the doctrines and traditions of men; but are willing to hear, and when they understand, obey the truth. Your devoted brother in Christ, J. H. Dunn.[72]

Dunn gave a picture that was prevalent in most of the surviving congregations across North Alabama. They all seemed to have problems. This was perhaps because most of the younger ministers were in the army, leaving the churches without spiritual guidance. Even the elders who were physically fit went off to war. Sad story after sad story can be found in personal letters, church records, and eventually post-war journals tell stories of how this situation developed in the Southern churches during the war.

A week later Dunn authored a favorable report on the work at Reunion. We give apportion of the report:

> ... I have just arrived at home from Reunion where I commenced speaking on Saturday evening and continued until last night, Tuesday I had respectable and attentive audiences up to the close. The results of our interview was, five additions; four confession, and one took membership in the congregation. Of the four two were males and two females. The congregation at Reunion is a noble band of disciples; the love of them aboundeth toward each other, this is especially true of the sisters. I never saw a more devoted sisterhood than those who worship at this place... Your brother in the one hope, J. H. Dunn.[73]

Three years later Granville held a successful meeting with the congregation at Reunion. After that meeting, the congregation invited David Lipscomb to come and preach to them. The request follows:

> Bro. Lipscomb: By the request of the Brethren at Reunion I write you a few lines asking you to attend. Our protracted

meeting which comes on Saturday before the first Lord's day in October. We have just had a meeting of several days and had 21 additions, two from the Baptists, several from the Methodists, some from the world, and some that had gone astray returned to the fold again.

Brother Granville Lipscomb was our preacher. The brethren are anxious for you to come and preach for us in October, if you can possibly do so. Your Brother in Christ, G. C. Vernon, Limestone County, Ala.[74]

In October David Lipscomb came and joined Granville Lipscomb at Reunion and conducted a gospel meeting. David Lipscomb reported on the meeting:

> On the first Lord's-day in Oct., we joined Bro. G. Lipscomb in a meeting at Reunion, near Athens, Ala. We remained until Tuesday afternoon. Up to the time of our leaving, there had been 15 or 16 additions, among the number an old. Lady who had been a seeker at the mourner's bench for forty years. Bro. Wm. Smith also came on Lord's day and remained until some days atter we left. The meeting was continued by Bro. G. Lipscomb, and we heard that up to Thursday morning there were thirty added to the faithful. D.L.[75]

David did more listening than preaching. He was mostly giving moral support to his nephew—Granville Lipscomb. His presence, however, encouraged the members at Reunion. Lipscomb was highly respected at Reunion.

The next report came from the pen of J. H. Dunn. He wrote:

> Bros. Lipscomb and Sewell: We commenced a meeting at Reunion, on last Saturday morning, and closed on Monday evening. The preachers in attendance were Bros. Pucket, Smith and me. The result was four accessions, Viz, one took membership, one reclaimed, two confessions, one immersion the other

to be immersed within a short time. Bro. Pucket was the principal speaker. who is "a host within himself." Much good. I fondly hope, will be the result of our meeting. Yours in the one hope, J. H. Dunn.[76]

This would be Dunn's last report on Reunion. Due to illness for the next ten years, J. H. Dunn made few trips to Reunion. He died July 10, 1877. Two years after Dunn's death, J. C. McQuiddy came to Reunion and held a meeting. He reported:

> J. C. McQuiddy writes from Athens, Ala, Sept. 13, 1879: I have just closed an interesting meeting at Reunion, seven miles northeast of Athens. I delivered fourteen discourses, resulting in twenty-three additions to the army of the faithful. Many more were "almost persuaded," yet they would not act. Man, how inconsistent thou art! Eternal life to be gained, eternal death to be avoided, still thou will not obey! The brethren at this place, desire preaching brethren to give them a call.[77]

From the statement made by McQuiddy—"The brethren at this place, desire preaching brethren to give them a call"—we can see that Reunion did not have regular preaching after Dunn's death.

Another report on the same meeting was sent to the *Gospel Advocate* by T. L. Weatherford. This report probably gives more information on the preacher and the congregation—thus we give it in full:

> Bros. L. & S.; Bro. J. C. McQuiddy of Farmington, Tenn., began preaching for the Big Creek congregation, and continued until Friday. The meeting resulting in 42 additions to the army of the faithful. The house would not hold the people on Lord's day, in fact, the house would not hold the people at any time during the meeting. Interest increased until the last, there being 9 baptized on the last day of the meeting; while at the water three came

forward and confessed the Savior, as did the Ethiopian officer, and were baptized. Truly it was a time of rejoicing with the brethren-to the Lord be all· the praise.

I would say (not intending to flatter our dear young brother and do not think it will) to the brethren, Bro. McQuiddy's schoolmates and dear teacher, that we have a remarkable young preacher in the person of Bro. McQuiddy. He is only twenty years of age, and notwithstanding his age he is, so to speak, a young walking Bible, with as much earnestness and zeal, we think, as we ever saw, especially in one so young. He not only preaches the gospel in its simplicity and beauty to the alien sinners, but he is excellent to instruct the brethren. On the last day of the meeting, he gave a noble lecture to the brethren, especially to the young converts. Bro. McQuiddy only has about a year's experience as a preacher.

The great good that is being accomplished in different parts of the country by M. H. B. C., is enough to encourage our much beloved Bro. Larimore to continue his labors in the Bible department. The good instructions given by Bro. Larimore during school months are now being scattered over the country. This should encourage brethren that are able to assist Bro. Larimore in his noble work. He is doing a great work and his work will increase for good in proportion to the interest taken by the brethren. Brethren, let us all work faithfully while it is day, for the night cometh when no man can work. Yours in the one faith, T. L. Weatherford. Near Athens, Ala., September 20th, 1879.[78]

A year later A. R. Crawford wrote of McQuiddy holding another meeting in August 1880, for the brethren at Reunion. The report was as follows:

A. R. Crawford writes from Athens, Ala., August 13, 1880: Bro. J. C. McQuiddy commenced a meeting with the congregation worshiping at Reunion, the second Lord's day in August, and closed the Friday following, which resulted in twenty-three additions to the church. The brethren were much built up and determined to press forward much more perseveringly in the future (than) in the past. To the Lord be all the praise.[79]

Crawford's report showed that the congregation there was making improvements in their spiritual life. They were growing in number, even without a regular preacher.

Our next mention of Reunion came in 1881. The *Athens Courier* published the schedule:

> T. L. Weatherford will preach at Mt. Rozel Academy on the 3rd Sunday in April, at 11 o'clock a.m.
> Re-Union—4th Sunday in each month, at 11 o'clock a.m.
> Shoal Bluff, Giles county, Tenn.—1st Sunday in each month at 11 a.m.[80]

Even though this was just a preaching schedule, it revealed just how busy Thomas L. Weatherford was at this time in his life. He had recently returned to Limestone County after being schooled at Larimore's Mars Hill College in Florence, Alabama.

Our next report in the *Gospel Advocate* came from Brother Thomas Nance. It was as follows:

> I left my home in this county yesterday was a week ago for old Reunion in Limestone county, Ala., to assist Bro. T. L. Weatherford in his meeting at that place and arrived there on Monday morning and owing to the scarlet fever in some families in the neighborhood and other surroundings, we thought it the part of prudence to close on Monday night. During the meeting there were two added by baptism and one from the sects... Thos. G. Nance, Minor Hill, Tenn., Oct. 10th, 1881.[81]

Brother Nance's report gave a picture of the hazards of preaching in those days. We could give an extensive list of gospel preachers who died from different diseases contracted while preaching in gospel meetings. This writer's Uncle J. R. Bradley contracted malaria while preaching in a meeting in North Mississippi. Nance and Weatherford were not only keeping themselves safe but perhaps all the people at Reunion.

Reunion was very saddened at the loss of a dear sister. Brother Weatherford reported the report:

> By request we give you the sad news of the death of Sister Kitty H. Riley, who departed this life April 27th. She obeyed the gospel at Big Creek several years past, moved her membership to Reunion, lived a faithful Christian life, and died in the faith. She left a mother husband, large family connection and a large circle of brethren, sisters, and friends to mourn her loss. May we all endeavor to meet her in the better land is the prayer of her brother in Christ. T. L. Weatherford.[82]

It would be another two years before any other news comes from Reunion.

B. C. Goodwin came and held a meeting in July of 1884. He reported:

> B. C. Goodwin, Elkmont, Ala., July 13, writes; I visited Reunion on the first Lord's day in this month, and there were two added to the army of the Lord, The church is in good working order there. I expect to hold them a meeting on the first Lord's day in October. Tell Bro. Barnes to send an appointment to Athens, Ala.[83]

The pages of the *Gospel Advocate* were silent, concerning Reunion, for seven years, until J. H. Morton came in 1891 and held a meeting at Reunion. Morton was from Marshall County, Tennessee, and was quite familiar with Reunion. He reported:

> Hyde, Oct. 16. '91.—Arrived here from Duck River, Tenn., Oct. 12. Joined Brother Curtis in a meeting at Reunion, Lime-

stone county. Result, eighteen additions, one from the Baptists and one from the Methodists. Preached last night to a large crowd under an arbor near this place. Preached 163 discourses since the last of July resulting in 167 additions to the good cause up to this writing. J. H. Morton.[84]

It would be another five years before another report came forth. This writer's great great-uncle J. R. Bradley came to Old Reunion in 1896 and held a good meeting. This was his first meeting for the year. J. R. was excited to be at the congregation where old Brother J.H. Dunn had worked for so many years. The meeting began on the fourth Sunday of July and continued through the first Sunday morning of August. J.R. wrote as follows:

> Booneville, Aug. 7: My meeting at Reunion, Limestone County, Ala., began on the fourth Sunday in July, and continued till the first Sunday In August. There was a good attendance and marked attention throughout the meeting [at Reunion]. I certainly think that the church is greatly strengthened spiritually by the meeting. There were twenty-one additions from all sources—twelve by confessions and baptisms, four took membership who had obeyed at other meetings, three from the Methodists, and one from the "Stephenites" (whatever that means).[85]

At Reunion, J.R. had probably preached to several who had been baptized by John Henry (J.H.) Dunn or had been encouraged by him. Reunion had been one of the key centers of the church in Limestone Co., Alabama for several years.

It was almost ten years until the next report came from Reunion. The report concerned a meeting held by Frank Morrow and Wilburn Derryberry. This meeting was successful. Derryberry authored an extensive report on September 11 which we give in full:

> I joined Brother Frank Morrow on the first Lord's day in September at Reunion, eight miles from Athens, Ala. We have had large crowds from the beginning. This has been a very pleasant meeting. The interest has been good all the time. To date (September 11) eleven have been baptized, three are to be baptized to-day, and six wanderers have confessed their wrongs. There have been many people baptized at Reunion. Quite a number of our older brethren have preached here in days gone by. According to Brother Pinkney Peace, who has lived here for years, I give the names of the following: Brethren D. Lipscomb, John Hundley, Granville Lipscomb, John Dunn, T. Fanning, Wade Barrett, T. B. Larimore, —Abernathy, J. K. Speer, J. H. Morton, T. L. Weatherford, Dr. Wallace, R. W. Officer, William Smith, James, Curtis. The congregation was organized about 1858. There are some earnest, zealous members here now. I go tonight to assist a few brethren about eight miles away in a meeting to be held in a new storehouse. Brother Morrow will remain at Reunion as long as the interest demands. W. Derryberry.[86]

This meeting made such an impression on Derryberry that he made a follow-up report near the end of September:

> Broadview, September 29. The meeting at Reunion, Ala., continued twelve days and closed, on Thursday night, September 14. There were sixteen baptisms, one of whom was a Methodist and one a Cumberland Presbyterian. One of those baptized was eighty-two years old. Two other Methodists and one Missionary Baptist who had been baptized also united with the church. Twelve wanderers confessed their wrongs and expressed a determination to live better. This was a pleasant meeting. Brother Morrow and I (Wilburn Derryberry) have agreed to go there again in 1907.[87]

They kept their appointment at Reunion the following year. Derryberry gave the report:

> Brother Wilburn Derryberry writes, under date of August 8: "Brother Frank Morrow and I recently assisted the brethren at Reunion, Ala., in a ten-days meeting which resulted in nineteen additions-ten were baptized, one from the Baptists, and eight restored. The audiences were very large throughout the meeting...[88]

Brother Derryberry was becoming quite popular in Limestone County by this time. It seems that Frank Morrow, also, had become popular among the churches in Limestone County. The following year it was not Derryberry and Morrow who came to Reunion, but Brother M. H. Northcross. He preached at Reunion in 1908. He gave a short report on his meeting. It was as follows:

> Brother M. H. Northcross made this office a pleasant visit last Friday. He was on his way to Totty's Bend, Tenn., where he is now engaged in a meeting. He recently held meetings at the following places: Reunion, Ala., with nine baptized, one from the Baptists, and four restored; Walnut, Miss., with two baptized; and Essary Springs, Tenn., with one restored.[89]

In 1909 Morrow returned and conducted another meeting. On this trip, he brought W. J. Johnson to aid in this meeting. The report was very short. It stated:

> Brethren Frank Morrow and W. J. Johnson recently closed a meeting at Old Reunion, Limestone County, Ala., with four baptized.[90]

In the same issue of the *Gospel Advocate*, Johnson sent his own report of the meeting:

... We began a meeting at Reunion, Ala., on the first Lord's day in August and continued it one week. As there was so much strife among the members, we devoted most of our time to preaching to the church. Two were baptized and two restored. W. J. Johnson.[91]

We usually do not give lengthy obituaries but the following obituary is worthy of being given in full. It not only reveals much about the person; but also gives considerable information relating to the congregational attitude towards the Lord's work at Reunion. The obituary reads:

> On September 20, 1909, the earthly pilgrimage or Sister Sophronie Peace came to a close. She was one of those who lived to do good. For about twenty years she was a member of old Reunion congregation, one of the oldest in North Alabama. One of the members who had been intimately acquainted with her for a number of years said: "One of Reunion's best members is gone." This church, like others, has had its troubles. but it was said of Sister Peace that she was never connected with any of their difficulties. She will be missed in the church, in the neighborhood, and in sickness. At the time of her death, she was the only one of the children living with her parents, who are growing feeble with years, and so she is sadly missed in the old home. She told loved ones around her not to mourn and weep, for she was going to heaven. She said she was not afraid of the journey. The large audience that gathered at the old meetinghouse on the day of burial and the tears that flowed testified much as to her past life. She was about thirty-eight years old. Her father was a member of Reunion Church. perhaps from its beginning, and his home was the preacher's home for many years; and a number of them, when they read this. doubtless will be ready to bear witness of the hospitality of that home while Sister Peace helped to provide for the comfort of those who were preaching the gospel to the people of that community. Quite a

number of those who have preached here too, have gone on before. When death comes, what a grand thought to look back over a Christian life, and what a miserable failure for the millions who refuse to accept Christianity! W. Derryberry. Athens, Ala. [92]

Derryberry described one of Reunion's best examples of what a Christian ought to be. This sister lived up to her name—Peace. He said she never took part in the quarrels that took place at Reunion from time to time. He also pointed to the fact that her father was most likely a charter member at Reunion. The family played host to a great number of preachers who came to Reunion. If the rest of the congregation had been like the Peace family, it would have been the brightest star among the North Alabama churches.

Derryberry returned to Reunion in October of 1910 and held another meeting. He described the progress of the meeting in the *Gospel Advocate* of November 3rd:

> Brother Wilburn Derryberry writes from Athens, Ala., under date of October 13: I recently closed a week's meeting at a schoolhouse five miles from this place, with good attendance and interest. but no additions. I am now in a meeting at Reunion, one of the oldest churches in North Alabama. Good attendance and interest growing. One is to be baptized today. The meeting is four days old and will continue as long as the interest demands. To-date there have been over a hundred added to the church in this (Limestone) county this year. [93]

He gave the results of the meeting a week later:

> Brother W. Derryberry of Athens, Ala., writes: At my appointment at a schoolhouse about twelve miles from Athens last Sunday afternoon two pairs of twin sisters made the confession, and I had the pleasure of baptizing them in Piney Creek

yesterday at about eleven o'clock. There is only seven days difference in their ages-sixteen years old last June. I baptized a brother of two of them a week before. The meeting at Reunion closed with six baptized and two restored. Church work seems to be on rising ground in this county this year.[94]

The church seemingly was beginning better times during this second decade of the twentieth century. Maybe this was a sign that this century would see Reunion get stronger. We shall wait and see! Wilburn Derryberry would hold one more meeting before our time limit on Limestone County expires. His report was actually two reports. One was the beginning of the meeting and the second was about the final results of the meeting. His first report read:

... I am now in a meeting with Reunion, one of the oldest churches of North Alabama. The meeting began last Sunday, and there has been one baptism to date. with six to be baptized today. Large crowds are in attendance. I am to begin a. mission meeting next Lor"s day about seven miles from the present meeting. W. Derryberry.[94]

His second report on this meeting stated:

Brother Wilburn Derryberry writes from Athens, Ala. The meeting at Reunion closed with sixteen baptized, one from the Baptists, and two restored. On Sunday afternoon, August 20, we had our first service in the new meetinghouse where the arbor meeting began on Saturday night before the fifth Sunday in July. They begin with about forty members.[96]

Our next report came from J. R. Bradley in August 1912. He announced that he was coming to Reunion on the first Sunday of September. His note read:

> Kelso, Tenn., July 28.-I will begin a meeting at Elkwood, Ala., on the third Sunday In August; at old Sharon, Ala., the first Sunday in September; at Reunion, Ala., the third Sunday in September; at Holland's Gin, the first Sunday in October; and at the Elk Cotton Mills, Fayetteville, Tenn., the fourth Sunday In October. These are all the meetings I have promised. Pray for us. -J. R. Bradley.[97]

J. R. Bradley, of Fayetteville, Tenn., held the next two meetings at Reunion. His report was published in the Advocate in October 1912. The *Gospel Advocate* stated:

> Brother J. R. Bradley, of Fayetteville, Tenn., sends the following interesting report...Our fourth meeting began on the third Sunday in September at Reunion, Ala., and closed on the fourth Sunday, with one baptism, one from the Baptists, and four restored. We held a meeting at Reunion sixteen years ago and baptized twenty-one. At our recent meeting there we had large crowds all the time... J. R. Bradley.[98]

Bradley would do considerable work in Limestone County and helped establish several congregations, much of which was done with T. L. Weatherford. An example: Bradley was back in Limestone County; but not just at Reunion. He participated in new works also. The following report shows just how much he participated in the county, as well as Reunion:

> Athens, Ala., September 22.-Our meeting, beginning the first Sunday in this month, which was announced to be held at "Old Sharon," had to be moved two miles below Sharon, near a Baptist church called "Charity." We preached fourteen times in a nice grove, once in the Charity Baptist Church, twice in the Kellogg Schoolhouse, once in the "Light" Schoolhouse, and closed with ten baptized, eight from the Baptists, and two from the Methodists, all claiming their baptism was to obey God, was to

get into Christ. I am at Reunion now. Pray for us. J. R. Bradley.
[99]

C. E. W. Dorris would close out our history of the Reunion church of Christ. His report was very short and to the point:

> C. E. W. Dorris, Totty's, Tenn., eighteen additions; Reunion, near Athens, Ala., six additions.[100]

This closes the "Old Reunion" history through 1914. In 2024 the congregation is still fighting the good battle and is the oldest congregation in Limestone County still meeting.

The Big Creek Group of Churches

It seems there were multiple congregations at different times and different places that were located on Big Creek, and in the same vicinity. They were simply referred to as Big Creek—they however were called by specific names by the locals. James R. Bradley spoke of two of these congregations when he came to Big Creek in 1897. He wrote:

> Minor Hill, Aug. 9. Our meeting at Big Creek, Ala., closed Friday night, with sixteen additions from all sources. It continued for a week at the "Shanghai" Schoolhouse, on the north side of the creek; the second week, just of night, at the Pleasant Point Schoolhouse, on the south side. There are several brethren and sisters accessible to both these schoolhouses. I think they ought to build a house of worship. The schools hinder the meetings at these schoolhouses, and the meetings hinder the schools. Brother T. L. Weatherford was with us just one day. He had a meeting of his own at another place. J. R. Bradley....[101]

When J.R. said the brethren should "build a house of worship" he obviously meant one house for the brethren of both communities to use, in other words, a joint effort. He did say that there were several "brethren and sisters" close to both locations. J.R. was a practical man and he knew that the church would do much better in a building of their own, under their control. J.R. had developed a great respect and love for the Limestone County brethren and loved preaching in that county. He had already preached at other locations around the Athens area.

As has already been discussed, Asa Plyler wrote about a document prepared by brother A. J. Rollings, who had lived and preached among the churches of that county for several years. This sketch gave some of the early history of the church in Limestone county.[102] It also gave the earliest documentation on this grouping of the Churches of Christ near Big Creek. Rollings wrote of this group:

> ... The third congregation of the Church of Christ, as far as can be learned, was the one that worshiped near the present location of the Shanghai public school. The church meeting here dispersed about 1900 and several new congregations were formed in that part of the country as the church grew. An old record, dating back to the beginning at Shanghai, has been found, and the following quotation is taken from the first page: "We whose names are hereunto subscribed being very desirous to maintain the ordinances of the House of God do congregate ourselves together and agree to meet at the school house near A. J. Weatherford's for that object taking the Bible and the Bible alone as the main of council for faith, rule and practice. This is the 3rd Lord's day in August 1861."
>
> There follows a list of some 500 names of those who were baptized for remission of sins during the course of the life of the Church of Christ at Old Shanghai. The quotation above will give an idea of the purpose in the hearts of these old pioneers. Also included in the record are accounts of withdrawal from those who walked disorderly after obeying the Gospel.[103]

The A. J. Weatherford mentioned above was baptized sometime in the 1840s, at Green Hill, before that work ended there. His wife was baptized by Allen Kendrick in 1843, at Green Hill. This congregation was the nearest congregation to the Weatherfords, prior to the establishment of the congregation near A. J. Weatherford and mentioned by A. J. Rollings in Plyler's book. This makes one wonder when Green Hill disbanded if it became a part of the Big Creek group. We pose this question since the Weatherfords were associated with Green Hill, maybe others who lived near the Weatherfords were a part of the Green Hill congregation also. These same people would have been in the group that established the Shanghai church in 1861.

From the reference to this record, we learn that this work began as the Civil War was beginning. It is amazing that this work grew stronger in faith and work during the war. Since, at the time, J. H. Dunn seemed to be the only gospel preacher living in Limestone County, he was most likely the preacher to have helped establish this congregation. Dunn was the first person to report, in a journal, on any kind of work on or near Big Creek. His report came as a one-line statement: "Bro. Dunn reported eight confessions at Big Creek."[104] Dunn interacted with the Big Creek work throughout the rest of his life. Dunn began preaching in this area in Limestone County in 1848.[105]

The next reference came from a William Smith of Giles County, Tennessee. We give the report:

> Bros. L&S. Brother G. Lipscomb and myself closed a meeting of six days labor including the first Lord's day in this mouth in Limestone County, North Alabama, five or six miles North-West of Athens, at Big Creek church, which resulted in twenty-three additions to the church of this number there were three from the Baptists, two from the Methodists, two from the Cumberland Presbyterians and four restored ...Yours in the one faith William Smith, Bethel, Giles Co., Tenn.[106]

Here again is the vague reference to the Big Creek church. We know of the two earliest works—Shanghai and Pleasant Point—being included in the journals as the Big Creek church. J. R. Bradley confirmed this suspicion in his 1897 report on the Big Creek work. Bradley spoke of both congregations being enough to build one house of worship. He said that there were several "brethren and sisters accessible to both these schoolhouses—Shanghai and Pleasant Point."[107]

Our next glimpse of the work on Big Creek came from H. J. Spivey of Lynnville, Tennessee. He seemed to be jubilant when he wrote:

> Brethren, L. & S: We held a meeting with the brethren at Big Creek, including fourth Lord's day in this month. The visible result was as follows: 23 additions by confession and baptism, 4 from the Baptist, 10 restored, 5 who had been withdrawn from by the Big Creek congregation, 5 from various other congregations. We met with and formed the acquaintance of a number of brethren that we had never seen before, among the rest was Old father Dunn, J. M. Curtiss, we also had the assistance of William Smith of Shoal Creek, Giles County, an earnest worker for the Lord. In a word, we never met more generous, warm-hearted brethren and sisters than those of Limestone Co. Ala. To the Lord be the Praise. Yours in Christ, H. J. Spivey. Lynnville, Aug. 30th, 1874.[108]

Sometime during 1874, Thomas L. Weatherford preached his first sermon and it was at Big Creek.[109] M. E. Terry revealed this bit of information about Weatherford's first sermon.

Our report relating to the Big Creek work came in the form of an obituary. It reported the death of J. H. Dunn's wife, Nannie C. Dunn. She had been a member at Big Creek for some time. T. L. Weatherford wrote the announcement:

Died of bilious fever Aug. 13th. 1875, Sister Nannie C. Dunn, wife of Elder J. H. Dunn, aged 56 years. 1 month. and 13 days. Sister Dunn was intelligent, pious, devoted, zealous and benevolent. She was beloved by all who knew her. Her seat among the disciples of Christ was never vacant when it was possible for her to be there. The church at Big Creek has lost a useful member whose place will not be easily filled. Bro. Dunn, who was a pioneer in the Reformation and is now 78 years old, is deprived of the counsel and the comforting influence of a beloved and loving companion. Dear sister, your brothers and sisters will join you one by until we all are landed safely on the other shore, T. L. Weatherford.[110]

Her husband J. H. Dunn would follow her in death two years later. Later in the year J. H. Holbrook came to Big Creek and held a gospel meeting. Weatherford reported the meeting:

T. L. Weatherford near Athens, Ala., writes: "There were eight immersions at our recent meeting. Bro. J. H. Halbrook did most of the preaching. He is a workman that need not be ashamed, and I can say the brethren are not ashamed of him. Brethren Curtis and Dunn were also with us."[111]

The meeting was a success and Big Creek showed signs of vitality. Brother Dunn was having health issues and made an appeal to the brethren for aid. He was now almost incapacitated and needed help. The following is his appeal:

The following extract we give from a recent letter from Bro. J. H. Dunn, of Athens, Ala.: If the brethren will continue their contributions, they will keep me and my little family (only three of us) from want—they have done nobly, for which my head is drawn toward them in gratitude. Should I not cross the dark river soon, I hope some friend will remind the brotherhood that their old brother and servant of the Lord is lingering near its banks and needs their help.[112]

In October H. J. Spivey of Lynnville, Tennessee, returned to Big Creek in a gospel meeting. T. W. Weatherford made the report:

> T. L. Weatherford writes from Athens, Ala.: Bro. Spivey commenced a protracted meeting Saturday night before the fourth Lord's day in August, at Big Creek church and continued until Friday. The following was the result—16 from the world, 4 from the Baptist, 4 from the Methodist, 1 immersed the week that the meeting commenced- 25 in all. Bro. Spivy is a noble workman io the Lord's cause. The brethren cannot do better than employ him if they want a good preacher. Bro. Curtis was with us and aided much.[113]

It may be noted here that J. H. Dunn was absent from his home church's meeting. By this time, he was bed fast. There was, however, joy spread up and down Big Creek about the success of this meeting. Everything was looking up.

By July of '77 Big Creek was in mourning. Sad news spread across North Alabama—the old pioneer preacher was dead. J. H. Dunn had died. We do not know who reported it to the *Gospel Advocate*. Someone at the *Gospel Advocate* must have written what was published. The obituary was very short for a man such as Brother Dunn:

> We have received advice of the death of that aged preacher and true soldier of Christ, Bro. J. H. Dunn. He died like he had lived, in the service of his Master. While preaching at the Big Creek Church near Athens, Ala.., the 2nd Lord's day in June, he fell prostrate in the stand and after lingering until that day he was called home to his reward. A suitable obituary notice of this truly good and pious man will appear shortly.[114]

Dunn had been living in that area of the county for some time. He had preached for several years along Big Creek. It was fitting that he should be stricken down in the pulpit while preaching at Big Creek to the people whom he loved so much, and no better place to end his life of service to the Lord than among those precious souls.

T. L. Weatherford gave our next glimpse at Big Creek in the form of a report on a meeting that J. C. McQuiddy held in September 1879. The report was lengthy and informative. The following extract demonstrates:

> Bros. L.&S.; Bro. J. C. McQuiddy of Farmington, Tenn., began preaching for the Big Creek congregation, and continued until Friday, the meeting resulting in 42 additions to the army of the faithful. The house would not hold the people on Lord's day, in fact, the house would not hold the people at any time during the meeting. Interest increased until the last there being 9 baptized on the last day of the meeting; while at the water three came forward and confessed, the Savior, as did the Ethiopian officer, and were baptized. Truly it was a time of rejoicing, with the brethren —to the Lord be all the praise. I would say (not intending to flatter our dear young brother and do not think it will) to the brethren, Bro. McQuiddy's schoolmates and dear teacher, that we have a remarkable young preacher in the person of Bro. McQuiddy. He is only twenty years of age, and notwithstanding his age he is, so to speak, a young walking Bible, with as much earnestness and zeal, we think, as we ever saw, especially in one so young. He not only preaches the gospel in its simplicity and beauty to the alien sinners, but he is excellent to instruct the brethren. On the last day of the meeting, he gave a noble lecture to the brethren, especially to the young converts. Bro. McQuiddy only has about a year's experience as a preacher...Brethren, let us all work faithfully while it is day, for the night cometh when no man can work. Yours in the one faith,

T. L. Weatherford. Near Athens, Ala., September 20th, 1879.
[115]

The results of this meeting were a testimony to the kind of preaching McQuiddy was capable of doing. It was also a testimony to the open-mindedness that the people of Big Creek possessed. Forty-two souls rescued during one meeting sounded almost like the old camp meetings of days gone by. Weatherford was overjoyed at the results.

In 1880 Robert Wallace Officer and a friend of his came through Big Creek on a preaching tour. They stopped and preached but we do not know of any results.[116] Later that year McQuiddy returned for another meeting. This time he brought a friend. T. C. Weatherford gave the report as follows:

> T. C. Weatherford writes from Rural Hill, Tenn., September l, 1880: Bro. G. W. Farris and J. C. McQuiddy began preaching on Saturday night before the fifth Lord's days — 5th Lord's day in August, at Big Creek, Ala., and continued day and night up to Friday, with large attendance. It resulted in twenty additions, seventeen Baptized, two from the Baptists and one from the Methodists. The brethren did good service, presenting the gospel clearly and simply to the alien, and also gave the brethren good lessons on Christian duty. Bro. J. C. McQuiddy's address is Winchester, Tenn., and Bro. Farris Maxwell, Tenn.[117]

This second meeting resulted in 20 souls coming to the Lord. That was less than half of the number that responded in McQuiddy's first meeting but that was still a great result for Big Creek. The only report from Big Creek was an obituary. T. L. Weatherford reported the sad news:

> Bro. S. A. Myers of Big Creek congregation departed this life October 25th. Bro. Myers was born in Limestone county, Ala., June 14th, 1864, obeyed the gospel under the preaching of Bro.

J. C. McQuiddy, September 1879, lived a faithful Christian life as far as known to the writer, passed away in the bloom of youth- we trust to a far better and happier land than this. T.L. Weatherford.[118]

It is noted that Brother Myers was baptized by McQuiddy during his first meeting at Big Creek. In October 1884 Sallie Terry, a sixteen-year-old girl wrote to Minor Metcalfe, one of the editors of the *Gospel Advocate,* and gave more information on Big Creek. Her home congregation was Shanghai. The note stated:

> Dear Uncle Minor: I assume the opportunity of writing to you for the first time. I am a little girl, sixteen years old, and have been a member of the church of Christ for three years. I go to Sunday school every Lord's day. Bro. William Smith preaches for us at Shanghai church seven miles west of Athens, every second Lord's day, and Bro. Wallace on the fourth.... Sallie Terry, Athens, Ala,[119]

The next meeting reported at Big Creek was not until 1888. Thomas G. Nance of Athens, Ala., held a meeting in connection with Brother T. L. Weatherford, at Big Creek. Nance reported 27 being added to the church at Big Creek.[120]

1889 began with sadness at Big Creek. One of their dear sweet sisters was promoted to eternal life. Her obituary was a touching report to all who lived along Big Creek. It was written by T. L. Weatherford as published below:

> Died, Jan. 7, 1889; Sister Elmyra Myres, aged 66 years, 3 months and 7 days. Sister Myres was born in one of the Carolinas May 15, 1818. Maiden name Henderson; joined the Missionary Baptist Church about 1858, united with the church of Christ at Big Creek, Limestone Co, Ala., about 1879. She loved the truth, was loved by the brethren and sisters that knew her, died in the faith and is reaping the Christian's reward. Sister Myres left two

children behind, six preceded her. If any of the connection or sisters see this write to J. W. Myers, Cartwright, Alabama. T. L. W.[121]

Sister Myers united with the church on Big Creek 11 or 12 years after it was established. J. H. Dunn would have been the key preacher at the time of becoming a member at that place. He may even have baptized her. In the fall of the following year a meeting was held by Brethren T. L. Weatherford and Wm. Jackson. Their report was given in the *Gospel Advocate* as follows:

> Brethren T. L. Weatherford and Wm. Jackson commenced a meeting at Potter Springs church on Saturday before the second Lord's day in this month. Bro. N. B. Wallace preached on Lord's day. I visited them on Wednesday and the brethren left the next day. I continued until Tuesday night after the 3rd Lord's day with nine added, seven baptisms and two reclaimed. Wednesday after the 3rd Lord's day I went to Brook's schoolhouse where Brethren Weatherford and Jackson had been since Sunday before the 3rd Lord's day, and while there preached four times for them, immediate results of the whole meeting, three added, two baptized, one put off baptism on account of sickness. From here 1 went to Shanghai church the home of Bro. Weatherford and Jackson and began preaching on the 4th Lord's day and preached until Thursday night only of nights with twenty added, eighteen by baptism. twelve by commendation. I did all the preaching while I stayed. Bro. Weatherford continued the meeting. J. F. Love, Jr, Elkmont, Aug. 30, '89.[122]

It was two more years before another report came from Big Creek. A meeting of two days was conducted by J. H. Morton of Belfast, Tennessee. T. L. Weatherford gave the report. It was a short report that read:

O'Neal, Nov. 21, '91. Bro. Jas. H. Morton, of Tennessee, preached three splendid discourses for us the 19th and 20th inst. Bro. Morton is a fierce defender or the gospel, knows how to preach it, and preaches it with great force. The brethren of Big Creek and Bethel have employed him for a protracted meeting: fifth Lord's day in July at Big Creek, and Bethel first Lord's day In August. T. L. Weatherford.[123]

Brother M. E. Terry of Cartwright, Limestone County sent the first report for 1892. It was informative. It gave a glimpse into T. L. Weatherford's life. Terry wrote:

Cartwright, August 8, '92. I write to you to inform you of the glorious meeting held at Shanghai, which was conducted by Bro. T. L. Weatherford. There were seventeen added by immersion, one from the Methodists, one from the Baptists, and two reclaimed. Bro. Weatherford preached his first sermon at this place eighteen years ago. (1874). He was born, raised, and obeyed the gospel at this place, and has always been a consistent and worthy member. M. E. Terry.[124]

Here we learn the approximate time Weatherford began preaching and the area in which he grew to manhood. Seventeen souls were added to the congregation at Shanghai. J. H. Morton had promised to conduct meetings, at this time, at Big Creek and Bethel, but was hindered by the progress of a meeting at Totty's Bend, Tennessee. He knew the brethren in Limestone County were disappointed, so he wrote the following:

Bluff Point. August 18,' 92. —We failed to reach our appointments in Alabama at Big Creek and Bethel on account of the good interest in a meeting at Tottey's Bend, Tenn.... If brethren at Big Creek and Bethel Ala., have gotten over their disappointment and are willing to make friends with me and desire it, I will visit them in September or October. I will, the Lord willing, be at Little Lot, 3rd Lord's day in August, Wilson Hill 4th Lord's day in August, and Shady Grove first Lord's day in September. J. H. Morton.[125]

No report was ever found on Morton holding a meeting for that year at Bethel. He did, however, come to Big Creek. Morton wrote of that meeting:

> Madison Sta., Oct. 2,'92. —Preached six days at Big Creek, resulting in nine additions. J. H. Morton.[126]

The brethren at Big Creek did use Brother Morton in several meetings. They did not hold a grudge against Morton. He returned to the Big Creek area in September. Weatherford wrote of that meeting:

> O'Neal, Oct. 4, "98.—Bro. J. H. Morton, of Tennessee, began a meeting at our home church on the 4th Lord's day in September, and closed with eight additions. Bro. M. is a good gospel preacher. Every discourse is strong and to the point. Thirty-one additions to the home work this fall. Three baptized near Center Star 3rd Lord's day, and one at Lexington, Lauderdale County, 4th Lord's day of September. These are new points that I have been working on at some point this year. To the Lord be all the praise. T. L. Weatherford.[127]

The work on Big Creek was still progressing in both churches —Shanghai and Pleasant Point. Morton returned to Big Creek in 1893. His report on this meeting was published on August 24, 1893. It gave the names of some of the older preachers from Limestone County who attended the meetings:

> O'Neal, August 15. We are now preaching at Big Creek, Ala. There were four confessions on the first Lord's day of our meeting. There have been eight additions at this writing. Brothers

Wm. Smith, N. B. Wallace, and Brother Wilson were present on the first Lord's day of the meeting. These are all preachers of the word. Brothers Smith and Wallace have grown old in the service, and their rest will be all the sweeter "some sweet day" for having fought a good fight. J. H. Morton.[128]

Morton had known these men for many years. It was refreshing to him to see these old soldiers of the cross come and support his efforts. Up until the time of Morton having authored this report, there had been eight additions as a result of his preaching. Before the meeting ended, the total number of additions was twelve.[129] Weatherford was not present at this meeting. He had gone to Texas on a six-week preaching tour. Upon his return, he wrote:

> O'Neal, September 1, I am home from a six-week stay in Texas. I met many good brethren and sisters there. Four additions to Big Creek church since my return. I go to help the brethren of Bethel the second Lord's day, and to Brooks' the third Lord's day in this month. T. L. Weatherford.[130]

Uncle Tom Weatherford, as T. L. was affectionately known among his friends, began 1894 by marrying a young couple at Big Creek. They were Ed Wooldridge and Fannie Terry. They were both members at Big Creek. The following year W. H. Sanday, a young preacher just beginning his preaching career, came to Big Creek and held a meeting. He was collaborating with Brother Weatherford. Sanday reported:

> Anderson's Creek, August 24.-My first protracted meeting for this season was held at Shoal Bluff, Tenn., and lasted five days, with six added. From there we went to Big Creek, Ala., and began there the fourth Lord's day in July, and continued seven days, with ten added. This place is near O'Neal, the home of our much-esteemed brother, T. L. Weatherford, and we can truly say

that this is one preacher that is not without honor in his own country. We then went from Big Creek to Bethel to assist Brother Weatherford in a meeting there, which lasted eight days, with twenty-tour added... W. H. Sandy.[131]

The first report for 1896 was from Weatherford who sent another obituary to the *Gospel Advocate* from Big Creek. It told of the death of Sister Nancy E. McCulley who had been a member at Big Creek since 1874.[132] She had been a member there for twenty-two years. In August J. H. Morton was supposed to have returned to Big Creek for another meeting. Morton wrote: "I will commence a meeting at Big Creek, Ala., on Friday night before the second Lord's day in August..."[133] He was hindered from coming and J. R. Bradley came in Morton's place. Bradley wrote of this:

> On the first Sunday night, after preaching twice at Reunion, I began at Big Creek (same county) in Brother Morton's place. I preached seven sermons and had eleven confessions and baptisms. Brother Hardy had one on Sunday, making twelve baptisms. Three were restored, making fifteen added at this place. I think that the brethren aim to get Brother George Waggoner, of Indiana, to continue this week. I had to come home and will begin at Chestnut Ridge tomorrow. J. R. Bradley. [134]

J.R. was just "filling in" for brother Morton (J.H.). Brother Morton was sick or tied up in another meeting and could not get free. It does seem, however, that J.R. was convenient to the location and was glad to take Brother Morton's place. All turned out well. His new Indiana friend, George Waggoner, would take over the meeting when he (J.R.) went home.

In October of 1896 T. L. Weatherford's father died. He was one of the charter members of the Shanghai-Big Creek work. His obituary is given in full below:

Died at his home in Limestone County, Ala., August 31, 1896, Elder A. J. Weatherford, at the advanced age of eighty-three years, two months, and sixteen days. Truly a good man has been called to his reward. Having lived a consistent member of the church of Christ more than fifty years, well could he exclaim, in the language of the Apostle Paul: "I have fought a good fight; I have finished my course; I have kept the faith." In the death of Brother Weatherford, the Big Creek church has lost one of its strongest pillars, and the community a noble Christian neighbor. The funeral services were conducted by Brother Bradley, at the Berea Cemetery, in the presence of a large concourse of relatives and friends, where he was laid to rest by the side of his faithful companion, there to await the resurrection of the saints. S. F. McGlocklin. Oneal, Ala.[135]

It may be noticed that J. R. Bradley conducted the funeral. He and T. L. Weatherford had been friends since they were students at Mars Hill Bible College.

In 1897 J.R. held more meetings in Limestone County, Alabama. His next two meetings were held in the Big Creek group of churches. His first meeting was on Big Creek, on the north side of the creek at "Shanghai" Schoolhouse. The second meeting was on the south side of Big Creek at the Pleasant Point Schoolhouse. Bradley thought that the brethren in both communities should build a house of worship for themselves. He wrote:

Minor Hill, Aug. 9. Our meeting at Big Creek, Ala., closed Friday night, with sixteen additions from all sources. It continued for a week at the "Shanghai " Schoolhouse, on the north side of the creek; the second week, just of nights, at the Pleasant Point Schoolhouse, on the south side. There are several brethren and sisters accessible to both these schoolhouses. I think they ought to build a house of worship. The schools hinder the meetings at these schoolhouses, and the meetings hinder the schools. Brother T. L. Weatherford was with us just one day. He had a meeting of his own at another place… J. R. Bradley.[136]

When J.R. said the brethren should "build a house of worship" he obviously meant one house for the brethren of both communities to use, in other words, a joint effort. He did say that there were several "brethren and sisters" close to both locations. J.R. was a practical man and he knew that the church would do much better in a building of their own, under their control. J.R. had developed a profound respect and love for the Limestone County brethren and loved preaching in that county. He had already preached at other locations around the Athens area.

After J. R.'s 1897 report, it would be six years before another report came forth from the Big Creek area. It came from the pen of J. D. Jones. Jones told of his visit to Shanghai:

> On my way from this place to Shanghai Church, not far from Athens, I preached three times. I began a meeting for that church on Saturday night before the Second Lord's day in August and closed on the following Friday night, With eighteen additions. On the 3rd Lord's day in August 1 began a meeting at Pleasant Point. On Wednesday, the meeting was moved to Union Schoolhouse, on Florence road and continued till Friday night. Four persons were baptised during the meeting. I began a meeting at Reunion, Limestone County, on the fourth Lord's day in August. The following Saturday at the water. There were twenty-three additions during the meeting… J. D. Jones.[137]

One can see that the Big Creek work was still viable, but still needed a spiritual boost. Jones gave a temporary boost to the congregations meeting as the Big Creek work. The work was in trouble, however. This can be seen in the next report which goes past our time frame for this essay. It is, however, needed to show how the work fared into the twentieth century. J. Clifford Murphy wrote that he closed a meeting at Shanghai on September

29, with ten baptisms. He explains that this meeting was a mission meeting. Things had happened to slow the work almost to a grinding halt. He stated: "This was a mission meeting, held mostly at the preacher's expense. The brethren promised to go to meeting on the first day of the week.[138] From this report, we can see that the church was not meeting on a regular basis. That was the reason Murphy got the members there to promise to meet every Lord's Day. The Big Creek's slow dissolution morphed into two new congregations in that section of Limestone County. This brings us to a close on the Big Creek work.

Mount Carmel

Adolphus Jackson (A. J.) Rollings' article, as recorded in Plyler's book, stated that chronologically, Mount Carmel Church of Christ was the next church to be established in the county. He wrote the following:

> Next in chronological order must have come the church at Mount Carmel. Records indicate that around 1880 Christians began to meet there and worship with no book but the Bible and wearing no name but Christ's.[139]

Dr. N. B. Wallace sent a report to the *Gospel Advocate* that is no doubt relating to the beginning work at Mount Carmel. It was reported:

> N B Wallace writes from Athens, Ala., October 17, 1879: We have had Bros. G. A. Farris and C. F. Gattis in our community for some days past, practicing dentistry in the day and preaching every night, Dr. Farris doing most of the preaching. He has done some excellent work; indeed, he has created quite an interest among the people here in behalf of Primitive Christianity. Seven Accessions already by confession and baptism, and the interest

unabated, one entire household of this number, father, mother and only child, (infant (sic) son some twenty years of age).[140]

Could this have been the beginning of the Mount Carmel work? This writer believes it is the beginning of Mount Carmel, due to the following documentation. We have one report from H. C. Abernathy of Giles County, Tennessee. He reported a six-day meeting in which he helped organize a congregation in Limestone County, Alabama. The details are tantalizing:

> I have just closed a series of meetings of six days in Limestone County, Ala.., resulting in thirty-one additions; ten from the Baptists, four from the Methodists; balance from the other part of the world. One Baptist preacher made the could good confession and goes on his way preaching the gospel in its purity. We organized a congregation of fifty-one members. we preached in the woods; had no house. We left too soon in midst of a good interest, would have had a grand success if I could have stayed longer, but had to leave to meet an appointment in the edge of Marshall county. We left the few scattering members that we gathered together greatly encouraged, and the new ones full of zeal; they are going to build a house right away. I preached at a neighbor's house on Thursday night before going to the above meeting and had four additions: three from the Methodists, one by confession. Still, they come. H. C. Abernathy, Minor Hill, Tenn., August 23, 1883.[141]

Maybe this was the beginning of Mount Carmel? We speculate that either Weatherford or Wallace or both had a hand in establishing Mt. Carmel but we have documentation that Bros. G. A. Farris and C. F. Gattis preached in Wallace's community before Abernathy's coming to that place, which Wallace identifies as "his community"[142] and home.[143] Abernathy said he organized a congregation; not establish one. There were twenty Christians in that vicinity, already. This group was already a congregation but not organized. Why did Abernathy not name it? It may have been because, at this time, there was no permanent place for worship. This being Mount Carmel, fits with Rollings' statement, that only six congregations were in existence before 1900.

Dr. N. B. Wallace drafted a lengthy report to R. W. Officer which was published in the *Gospel Advocate* in December 1883 under the title—"Letter To Bro. Officer." We give the entire report as it gives a good picture of things relating to Mount Carmel before it was organized:

> Bro. Officer expresses a desire to hear from me through the Advocate. In consideration of the high esteem in which I hold him, from a perfect knowledge of his uncompromising devotion to the truth as it, is in Jesus, and his indefatigable labor, "in season and out of season in all long suffering and doctrine, always abounding in the work of the Lord," I venture to risk this trespass upon the time and patience of the readers of the Advocate. I have no special theme in my mind but will write a sort of "general epistle." It is known to some of the brotherhood that Western Limestone has never afforded a very rich field in which to propagate the "ancient gospel" however, there are here a few of as loyal subjects to the king immortal as may be found anywhere, and with the assistance of these few we have a very neat comfortable house of worship, 28X40 feet. Seats lacking—hope soon to have them in place, and hope travelling brethren, when they pass this way will give us a call, and among all our travelling brethren, none would be more acceptable than Bro. R. W. Officer.
>
> We have never asked or received anything or anything of consequence from the Brotherhood or others in this work. It being the Lord's matter will take care of itself. The house is situated just 13 (12.2) miles west of Athens, in Limestone County Ala. There are within a few miles of the church the faithful few mentioned, a number of others who were once of us, but now seem to have forgotten their first love, and if they have any spiri-

tual life at all it is a sort of a quasi-vitality, only I fear; by their fruits ye shall know them. According to the divine rule if a professed Christian does not meet with the children of God on the Lord's day of the week when he can, to participate with his brethren in the glorious and heaven born principles of that day but let any trivial thing or nothing prevent him from doing so, contributes nothing to the furtherance of the cause, makes no sacrifices, and in short manifests by his conduct that he is not interested in his own salvation, nor in that of a perishing world, is evidently in a state of spiritual collapse, to nearly approaching "articulo mortis'" that a happy restoration is a very doubtful terminus of the case. But there was a catholicon (A remedy for all diseases) opened in the house of King David. A sure antidote to all sin and cleanness. Drs. Paul, Peter, James, and John, the beloved physician, and the whole line of worthies have left their affidavits in golden characters on the annals of time all along or down the ages, testifying that this is true, and through this is the indispensable, the "sinis" (taking away) of all human woes and sorrows, yet it is ignored by poor, perishing mortals, and in refusing to take the grand specific prepared in heaven's great laboratory, the only means of life eternal are rejected, and our sun must set in eternal night.

Paul says, "The just shall live by faith, but if any man draw back my soul shall have no pleasure in him." And the apostle Peter plainly teaches that those who fail, to do the things enjoined in the word of God "are blind and cannot see afar off, and hath forgotten that he was purged from his old sins." Might we not as well expect to gather "grapes from thorns or figs from thistles," as to find a Christian so blind that he can see no beauty in a hearty, cheerful obedience to God's requirements? A blind, live Christian is a nonentity.

In contemplating this apostasy from the practical duties of Christianity, one feels something like the captive Jews, when "they sat by the rivers of Babylon and wept when they remembered Jerusalem and hanged their harps upon the willows in the midst thereof." They could not sing the songs of Zion in a strange land. Christians must dwell in Gods house if they would sing his songs acceptably, and the song of the redeemed in the sweet by and by.

    I continue to do what preaching I can, which is at one place or another about every Lord's day; my labors are occasionally blessed with some valuable accessions to the army of the faithful. I am so pressed with the lack of zeal and self-sacrificing devotion among us as to hasten rather leisurely in making converts. I think it "meet as long I am in this tabernacle" to do what I can under God, both by precept and example, to stimulate a spirit of living devotion practical piety among my brethren, trusting that in its reflex action I may be strengthened and benefitted also. I have but one co-laborer near me Bro. T. L Weatherford who is truly a workman that need not be ashamed for he knows how to wield the sword of the spirit to the slaying of the mighty men of Gath. His voice can always be heard loud and shrill along the lines of the embattling hosts of Israel "onward to victory or death."

    And in conclusion, Bros. Robt. and Tom, let us ever be faithful ministers of Jesus Christ following implicitly the holy instructions given us in our Father's Book, "looking for the blessed hope and the glorious appearing of the great God and our Savior Jesus Christ. Yours in Christ. N. B. Wallace.[144]

In this letter, we read about a new house of worship being almost finished. We discover that Wallace only had one other gospel preacher living anywhere near him. That was T. L. Weatherford. Wallace was very close to R. W. Officer in friendship as this letter bears out. The whole western part of Limestone had seemingly lost its zeal, with a small exception. Wallace says that some had not left their first love.

    N. B. Wallace sent a report about a meeting but did not call the location by name. The first mention of Mount Carmel, by name, in the *Gospel Advocate*, was in 1883 in the report below. It was made by Dr. N. B. Wallace. It had good information on Mount Carmel, Wallace, and Robert Wallace Officer—missionary in Oklahoma. Below is the full report:

> Brother N. B. Wallace writes from Petty, Ala.: "I am still trying to preach the Jerusalem gospel. The father of all mercies surely is in this work. I preached on third Lord's day June at Mt Carmel (home) one discourse to a splendid audience, one in afternoon by Bro. T. L. Weatherford. Again, on first Lord's day, July, three miles from home to a very large audience, splendid attention, although the Methodists set up an opposition just one-half mile off, no doubt to interfere with the people hearing. Nevertheless, the result of these discourses, was one from the Baptists and nine by confession and baptism. To the Lord be all the praise. The outlook for the reformation here is fine now, better than at any former time. I am getting much worn, but by the grace of God I will preach as best I can the claims of King Jesus upon the people. God help us to be soul, mine, and strength in the great work, oh! for the faith and indomitable will of the heroes of the cross, who have preceded us. This seems to me to be the auspicious moment for the reformation, and instead of fretting our strength and resources away about things of no profit, bring about dissension, strife, and division. We ought to be of the same judgment, joined together in the same mind, speaking the same things, and a concerted move all along the line would give an impetus to the great work never seen before, since the apostolic day. Why not do it? Bro. Officer writes in a letter: thank the Lord. Send me one half dozen each Grub-Ax. Upset and Theological Pump Reset. I think Bro. K. did a finished job, and how the Brother wanting to make a respectable axe out of that rotten pewter edged thing I cannot divine."[145]

The information we hoped could be found—Who established Mount Carmel and when was it established? Thomas Weatherford gave the next tidbit of information in his appointment list for 1887. Weatherford had his appointments published in the *Gospel Advocate* for the year 1887, as follows:

> Bro, T. L. Weatherford's appointments for 1887 are as follows: Bethel, Brooks' Schoolhouse, Mt. Carmel, first, second and third Lord's days, respectively. All the points are in Limestone county, Ala.[146]

At the time these two reports were published, the church had already been established for some time. The establishment of the church at Mount Carmel is still a mystery. We know that Wallace lived in that community and Weatherford lived not far away. We also know that Farris and Gattis, and Abernathy had preached in this community. Who began the first efforts at preaching there? It is difficult to believe that neither Wallace nor Weatherford ever made the first efforts at establishing a work in that community, which was their community. We can only make speculations as to when and who. Weatherford's list containing Mount Carmel tells us that the church had already been established for some time.

The third mention of Mount Carmel in the *Gospel Advocate* was an announcement about a marriage by T. L. Weatherford. The report simply read:

> Married at Mt. Carmel, 3d Lords day in February, Ms. Alice Speer and Mr. Jno. Sides, all in Limestone county, by T. L. Weatherford.[147]

We do know that by March 1887 the church was already a viable congregation. The above report confirms that fact.

Our next report came from J. M. Hughes, a local resident and member at Mount Carmel. He gave us a very informative report below:

> J. M. Hughes writes from Petty, Ala.: "N. B. Wallace and T. L. Weatherford began a meeting at Mt. Carmel (Dr. Wallace's

home congregation) on Saturday night before the third Lord's day in August and continued three days, with seven added to the church. The brethren at this place seem to be in a good condition spiritually, and have a splendid house in which to worship, built mainly by Dr. Wallace. Bro. Weatherford began another meeting at Brooks' Schoolhouse on Friday night before the second Lord's day in September, and closed the following Wednesday night, resulting in nineteen additions to the King's army besides a great revival of zeal among the brethren. Bro. Wallace came over on Lord's day and preached two able discourses to large audiences. These two brethren are, indeed, true yokefellows in the gospel. May the Lord long preserve and bless them in holding out the blessed gospel to a dying world, is my prayer."[148]

In this report, we learn that Mount Carmel was still Wallace's home congregation and that the house of worship was mostly built by Wallace's efforts. It also suggested that Weatherford and Wallace had worked together as a team for a long time. Weatherford and Wallace are the only two preachers mentioned in the early days after Mount Carmel was given a name; therefore, we know that these two men played an important part in establishing this work and that Rollings' guess at the approximate time of establishment is fairly close. We do know that by March 1887 the church was already a growing congregation. The above report confirms that fact.

Four years later we get another report. This time it was written in 1891 and came from J. W. Lanier. He reported another meeting held by T. L. Weatherford, and it read as follows:

> Pettey, Sept. 14, '91. —Bro. T. L. Weatherford has just closed a very interesting meeting with us at Mt. Carmel. He delivered nine discourses, and the immediate results were thirteen baptized, four restored and four took membership. Bro. W. is a

workman that needeth not to be ashamed, rightly dividing the word of truth. To God be all the praise. J. W. Lanier.[149]

The Mount Carmel congregation was getting on a firm footing spiritually and numerically. Weatherford and Wallace continued to nurture the church at Mount Carmel. The congregation did a slight name change—from "Mt. Carmel" to "Mount Carmel." That is the way the name would appear in the *Gospel Advocate* from then forward. The next meeting reported was two years later. In July W. H. Sanday came and held a twelve-day meeting. The report is given in full:

> Pettey, Oct. 23. —I wish to report a most glorious meeting conducted by Brother W. H. Sandy, at Mount Carmel, which began the third Lord's day in July. The meeting lasted twelve days—twenty-two sermons in all. The meeting would have lasted longer but owing to so much sickness in the neighborhood he decided to close. Brother Sandy is a promising young man, and a very good preacher for his years. We had forty-eight additions by confession and baptism, ten from the sects, and five restored, and the brethren and sisters more alive to their duty than I have ever known them, Since this, Brothers Sandy and Brendle held us a few night services, which resulted in adding four more to the one body. J. C. Lecroix.[150]

J. P. Jones reported another meeting held by Sandy sometime in October at Mount Carmel. His report was dated—Lexington, Oct. 1. It read as follows:

> Lexington, Oct. 1.-Brother W. H. Sandy began a meeting here on the fourth Lord's day in last month, and preached ten times, closing Thursday night...Thence he went to Piney Grove; preached two discourses, and came home, to hold a meeting at Mount Carmel, Limestone county, Ala., which lasted six days, and resulted in four additions. He left an appointment for

Brother Underwood to continue the meeting at Piney Grove, Miss. J.P. Jones.[151]

Though Sandy was a young man he became very popular in North Alabama and Northeast Mississippi. He held several meetings before his health failed him.

With the two meetings mentioned above, the congregation was stirred to being more active and faithful. Within two more years (September 1895) W. H. Sanday announced that he was in a meeting conducted by T. L. Weatherford at Mount Carmel.[152] The final report on that meeting was given in the *Gospel Advocate* by Sandy in October:

> Anderson's Creek, Sept. 18. -Our meeting at Mount Carmel, Ala., conducted by Brother Weatherford and me, lasted five days, with eleven added. I then preached at Porter's Springs, near Rogersville, Ala., on Lord's day following, which was last Lord's day, and had twelve additions. The twelve added last Lord's day made sixty-one that have been added to the congregation at Oak Ridge in two weeks. W. H. Sandy.[153]

The church at Mount Carmel was growing toward maturity. Weatherford seemed to be the mainstay at Mount Carmel. He was the one that was always there in time of need. In 1897 he and J. P. (Dr. Paisley) Jones held a meeting at Mount Carmel. Weatherford reported on that meeting:

> Elk River Mills, Nov. 10.-Dr. Paisley Jones and I concluded a few days' meeting at Mount Carmel on the first Lord's day in October, with ten additions and some restored. There were two baptisms in the same week at my home. Brother Jones is a good brother to work with. No jealousy or preacherism. T. L. Weatherford.[154]

This meeting was very successful. It seems that neither

preacher received any remuneration for this meeting, and none was expected. That is why Weatherford quoted one of his old Mars Hill classmates—F. D. Srygley.

It seemed that Mount Carmel had been having a reported meeting on a two-year basis. It appeared that the preachers came and preached every two years based on the occurring reports; but the next report came twelve years later; it was sent to the *Gospel Advocate* from another young local preacher—J. Petty Ezell:

> Brother J. Felty Ezell recently held meetings at Antioch and Cross Roads, Lauderdale County, Ala., with no visible results; and on September 7, he closed a meeting at Mount Carmel, Limestone County, Ala., his home congregation, with nineteen additions-eleven baptized, seven restored, and one from the Baptists.[155]

Another two years passed without an inside look at Mount Carmel. A preacher from Lawrenceburg, Tennessee held a meeting. T. C. King was familiar to many North Alabamians. He had preached around Cullman and Morgan Counties for some years before moving to Tennessee. The report follows:

> Brother Thomas C. King baptized sixteen persons at Mount Carmel, Ala. The same number were restored. He is now at Smyrna Church, in Maury County, Tenn. Five have been baptized there.[156]

That meeting was a success. The people loved Brother King's preaching so much that they invited him back for another meeting the following year. King sent a short report on the meeting:

> Lawrenceburg, Tenn., August 2.-our meeting at Mount Carmel, Ala., closed on August 1. Eighteen persons (sic) were baptized and ten restored. Interest was good. -Thomas C. King.[157]

King returned for a third meeting in 1914. His success in the two prior meetings had won the hearts of the people at Mount Carmel. Sent a report on August 15, 1914, and another on August 20, 1914.[158] The meeting only lasted only five days due to the illness of his daughter back in Tennessee. He wrote of the abrupt ending:

> Lawrenceburg, August 20.-Our meeting at Mount Carmel, Ala., closed prematurely on account of the sickness of our daughter at home. The meeting continued only five days. Twenty-three were baptized. Fourteen confessed the last night of the meeting. Thomas C. King.[159]

King had helped to bring durability to the church at that place. Due to his work and the others before him, the congregation remains strong today (2024). J. Petty Ezell preached on the fifth Sunday of November 1914. He wrote of this:

> ... On the fourth Lord's day I preached at Aldridge Grove, at 11 A. M. and 7 P.M.; on the fifth Lord's day, at Mount Carmel, Limestone County, my old home...[160]

No other report followed up on Ezell's trip to Mount Carmel. This is the end of our designated time frame for our history of Limestone County, but a report two years beyond this time frame was so tantalizing that we put it in this history. We give it in full:

> I preached at Mount Carmel on Saturday night and Sunday, with one baptism and one restoration, and two from the Christian Church took membership with the church. The work there has grown much within the last few months and the church as a whole is becoming more and more interested.[161]

This report testifies to the continued growth of Mount Carmel. This writer attended Mount Carmel when he was in the second grade at Clements Elementary School. That was in 1950. The congregation was thriving very well at that time and still is. It has been a Christian haven for many souls, and we pray it may continue 'till the Lord returns. This closes the history of Mount Carmel.

Bethel

Bethel Church of Christ began in a log house located on Highway 72 about one mile east of our present location. This building burned over 100 years ago. From that location, the congregation met in a building on Mooresville Road about one mile south of Highway 72. On March 18, 1923, this building was destroyed by a tornado.[162] A.J. Rollings gave his version of the establishment of the Bethel congregation. Asa Plyler recorded this information from Rollings' manuscript as follows:

> The congregation meeting at Bethel began just a year or so later, probably in 83 or 84. There was first an old log house situated a short distance from the present location. This building burned and another erected just off the present Huntsville highway on the road leading to Mooresville. After this building was destroyed in a storm the present meeting house was erected.[163]

Rollings was giving an educated guess, which by the way, may be accurate. But we have to give what is recorded, to piece together an accurate history. The first mention of Bethel in the *Gospel Advocate* came from Franklin Pepper, a charter member at

Bethel. Bethel was already a congregation when he sent his report. The note read:

> Bro. Franklin Pepper writes: Dr. Wallace and T. L. Weatherford commenced a meeting at Bethel Limestone county Ala. on Saturday night before 5th Lord's day in August and continued eight days, resulting in thirty-three baptism, two from the Baptists, two reclaimed and one by commendation. Had large attendance. Bro. Wallace and Bro. Weatherford work together a great deal and get along harmoniously. They are excellent preachers and are doing a great work for the Master's cause in this part of the country.[164]

The above report makes Rollings' statement credible. Pepper sent the second documented report in 1886. It read:

> Bro. Franklin Pepper writes: "A meeting began on first Lord's day in September at Bethel, Ala., resulting in twenty-four additions to the church—nineteen by baptism, three from the Baptists and two reclaimed. The meeting was conducted by Bros. T. L. Weatherford and Dr. N. B. Wallace, assisted by Bros. Speegle and Wilhite, two young preachers from Morgan county. The preaching was excellent."[165]

From these first two reports, it appears that Weatherford and Wallace were the preachers who established the Bethel congregation. This makes sense since both men lived in Limestone County and were preaching at various mission points.

In January Weatherford had the *Gospel Advocate* publish his schedule for that year:

> Bro, T. L. Weatherford's appointments for 1887 are as follows: Bethel, Brooks' Schoolhouse, Mt. Carmel, first, second and third Lord's days, respectively. All the points are in Limestone county, Ala.[166]

Weatherford was well received at Bethel and was often called upon to perform weddings. One such wedding was performed in 1887:

> T. L. Weatherford writes from O'Neal, Limestone county, Ala., March 2nd, 1887: "Married, at the residence of the bride's mother, sister Seaney Ekebarger, Bro. Clinton Glaze, of Athene, to sister Annie Ekebarger, of Bethel, Limestone county, March 2nd."[167]

Not only does this reveal that the bride was from Bethel; but also reveals another family name at Bethel —"Ekebarger." Many other weddings are on record in the Limestone County Courthouse and are connected to Weatherford and Bethel.

That same year Bethel got mission-minded and sent two dollars to R. W. Officer, a missionary to the Indians in Oklahoma.[168] Weatherford also had his schedule published a second time in 1887. He wrote:

> "My regular appointments for the year are Bethel, on the first Lord's day; Brooks' Schoolhouse the second, and Mt. Carmel the third of each month. I reserve the fourth Lord's day to go to various places."[169]

Franklin Pepper wrote another report to the *Gospel Advocate*, also, reporting on a meeting by Weatherford and Wallace. In this report, he told of a third meeting by Weatherford and Dr. Wallace the report was as follows:

> Franklin Pepper writes from Athens, Ala., Aug. 19th: Bro. T. L. Weatherford and Dr. Wallace held us a meeting of four days duration at Bethel, Limestone county, Ala., with thirteen additions, 5 from the Methodists, 3 from the Baptists, 2 from the world, 3 took membership. This makes three protracted meetings held for us by these brethren, resulting in about 65 addi-

tions to the church. We number about 85. Brethren Weatherford and Wallace are excellent preachers and are doing a great work for the Master in Limestone and adjoining counties. [170]

This report gave commendatory information about the team of Weatherford and Wallace and how harmoniously they worked together. It also showed the power with which they presented the gospel in four nights with thirteen responses.

It would be two more years before the *Gospel Advocate* mentioned the work at Bethel. We know of nothing reported in any other source. Finally, a report appeared in 1889. It reported a wedding conducted by T. L. Weatherford at Bethel. We give the entire report:

Married, at Bethel, Limestone county, Ala., first Lord's day in May, 10 A.M., Brother W. T. Calvin and Sister Ophelia Thomas, all of Limestone county. Also, on May 9, 6 P. M., Mr. Hartman and Sister Collier, T. L. Weatherford officiating, at the residence of the bride's father, same county.[171]

So, the wedding happened in the home of the bride who lived at Bethel. This tells us that the community was referred to as "Bethel." Following a wedding announcement in the *Gospel Advocate* came a sad announcement. It was the obituary of one of the members at Bethel. It was Sister Eckerberger. Her death was reported by Dr. N. B. Wallace of Elkmont. It is recorded below:

It becomes my melancholy duty to announce the death of Sister Eckerberger, who passed "to that mysterious realm" at her home in Athens, Ala., July 21, 1890, aged 49 years, 2 months, and 10 days. She became a Christian in 1865; was married the year before to David Eckerberger, who died some fourteen years ago, leaving Sister E. with five little orphan children to care for, and be it said to her praise, well did she do it. Verily the Lord watches over the widow and the orphan. She was a member of the Bethel congregation, this county, where I often preached, and was often at her house, and well she knew how to make the preacher feel at home. Truly she was a mother in Israel. What a loss to the church, to society, and above all to the dear children. May God bless, comfort and sustain them in their irreparable loss, and may they imitate the example of their noble departed mother. How inscrutable are God's judgments, and his ways past finding out. N. B. W.[172]

The next September brings another report about Bethel:

At last reports Bro. H. F. Williams was engaged in a good meeting at Bethel, Limestone county, Ala. We have not learned the number of additions.[173]

A lengthy report followed the meeting:

Bethel Congregation, five miles east of Athens Ala., was also ripe and ready for a meeting. Of course, we had it beginning Saturday night before the 3rd Lord's day in August and continuing till the next Saturday. I preached fifteen discourses for them besides making several talks at the water. There were eight added. The brethren here number about eighty members, nearly all very poor in this world's goods, but in the main they are as fine specimens of living abiding faith as can be found. Here too the "amen" corners were filled and that too by young people mostly who took great interest in the singing and preaching. I have not observed better order and attention anywhere than here. It was a great delight to me to work with and preach for them. H. F. Williams.[174]

The next year Bethel expected J. H. Morton to come and hold a gospel meeting for them in August, but Morton was having such success that he extended the meeting in which he was engaged and missed his appointments at Bethel and Big Creek. He wrote the following explanation:

> Bluff Point, August 18, '92: We failed to reach our appointments in Alabama at Big Creek and Bethel on account of the good interest in a meeting at Tottey's Bend, Tenn. The cause of Christ seems to be gaining very rapidly in Hickman County; 115 soldiers were enlisted at Pinewood and forty-five at Warner, and meeting still being continued, Bros. Spicer and Meacham preaching "Jesus to the people;" Sixteen at Totty's Bend, seven at Cathcy's Creek, four at this writing at Bethel (Anderson's Bend.) If brethren at Big Creek and Bethel Ala., have gotten over their disappointment and are willing to make friends with me and desire it, I will visit them in September or October... J. H. Morton.[175]

Morton was a new face at Bethel. J. H. Morton of Belfast, Tennessee came in September of 1892 and began a meeting and Brother John Hayes of Limestone County finished the meeting. Morton's preaching yielded thirteen additions. We do not know the results of Hayes' preaching. It was noted that Hayes was still a student at "Nashville Bible School" (later called David Lipscomb College). Morton sent the report as follows:

> Athens, Sept. 16, '92. Began a meeting at Bethel, Limestone County last Lord's day: thirteen additions, five from the Methodists. Bro. Hayes, from the 'Nashville Bible School, formerly from California, will continue the meeting. J. H. Morton.[176]

The following year Weatherford made a preaching trip to Texas. Upon his return to Limestone County, he resumed his schedule for the rest of the year, which seemed an awful lot like his schedule for the last few years. Weatherford wrote a short report on his return:

O'Neal, Sept. 1. I am home from a six-week stay in Texas. I met many good brethren and sisters there. Four additions to Big Creek church since my return. I go to help the brethren of Bethel the second Lord's day, and to Brooks' the third Lord's day in this month. T. L. Weatherford.[177]

"Uncle Tom" sent a closing report on that meeting:

O'Neal, Sept. 17. —A few days' meetings at Bethel, the first Lord's day in September, resulted in five additions—three from the Methodists. Two days' and nights' meetings at Miss Alice John's schoolhouse resulted in thirteen additions—nine baptized three from the Baptists, and several from the Methodists. T. L. Weatherford.[178]

Another two-year interval before the next report on Bethel. This time T. B. Larimore came and held a gospel meeting. W. H. Sanday from the Rogersville area authored the report. It simply stated—We then went to Athens to hear Brother Larimore ... W. H. Sandy.[179]

Another new face came to hold the annual meeting. It was M. H. Northcross. He reported meetings in two locations:

Please announce through Gospel Advocate that Hopkinsville, Ky., will be my address for the next two weeks. I will begin a meeting (D. V.) at Bethel, near Athens, Ala., the first Lord's day in October; first Lord's day in November, at West End, Williamson County. M. H. Northcross, Franklin. Tenn., Sept. 20.[180]

In 1896 James R. Bradley came to Bethel and held a brush arbor meeting which was sponsored by the Bethel brethren. Bradley reported:

> We began on the first Sunday in this month at an arbor near Bethel, Limestone County, Ala., and closed on the second Sunday, with seven additions—four from the Baptists, two from the Methodists, and two reclaimed. This was the work of the Bethel brethren. J. R. Bradley.[181]

Was this an attempt to establish a congregation near Bethel or was the meeting for the benefit of the Bethel church? We do not get enough information to make a clear decision.

The Bethel reports have been coming, mostly, at two-year intervals. The next one was a couple of years later. M. H. Northcross returned in 1896 to Bethel and held another meeting. His report stated:

> I began a protracted meeting at Bethel, Limestone County, Ala., the first Lord's day in August, and continued one week, with ten added to an excellent band of disciples, who are worshiping after the ancient manner. M. H. Northcross.[182]

Little is known of Northcross. He was born in North Mississippi near the Tennessee state line. He lived and preached at Bunker Hill, Giles County, Tennessee for several years. He was acclaimed as a very good preacher. His visit to Bethel was profitable for the Bethel congregation.

Next year Franklin Pepper reported a meeting held by T. L. Weatherford and B. C. Goodwin. They preached one week at Bethel and at another location in a schoolhouse. Pepper wrote:

> Athens, September 18. We have had one of the best meetings at Bethel, Limestone County, that we have ever had. Brothers T. L. Weatherford and B. C. Goodwin did the preaching, except two sermons preached by Brother John Hayes. All three of these brethren are fine preachers. The meeting continued for two weeks—one week at Bethel and the other at a schoolhouse a few miles off. Brother Goodwin did all the preaching at the latter

place. There were twenty-two baptisms and two reclaimed. Franklin Pepper wrote.[183]

From this report forward the information becomes very scanty. It will be nearly a decade before any more information can be found on Bethel. J. T. Harrison, a young preacher came to Bethel and held a meeting. He announced his intentions to come and preach in August 1909.[184] The *Gospel Advocate* reported the results two weeks as "with eleven baptized and three restored."[185] The next year he returned to hold another meeting. His intentions were announced in the August 12th issue of the *Gospel Advocate*.[186]

Our last report for the time frame set forth is from Brother Wilburn Derryberry. It gave our last view of Bethel:

> ...I was away from the first Sunday till Friday night following, in a meeting with Bethel Church, in this county. with large attendance and one baptism. I am now in a meeting with Reunion, one of the oldest churches of North Alabama. The meeting began last Sunday, and there has been one baptism to date. with six to be baptized today. Large crowds are in attendance. I am to begin a. mission meeting next Lord's day about seven miles from the present meeting. W. Derryberry.[187]

Derryberry had preached for a few years at the Reunion congregation and had preached throughout Limestone County. He was no stranger to Bethel. He was very popular for the next few years at Bethel. In 2024 Bethel is the strongest country congregation, numerically speaking, and a leader in spirituality. They are very mission-minded and have good leadership. If Bethel continues as it is now it will continue to grow.

Athens

The church in Athens, as was the case in most North Alabama towns, was established much later than the rural congregations. The Christian Church history speaks of men preaching in Athens as early as the 1860s, but there is no documented evidence that this was the case. There were a few Christians who lived in Athens; but no congregation had been documented. Tolbert Fanning traveled through Athens on a train and describes the war damage he saw, but never mentions a church house or a gathered congregation in Athens. He wrote the following:

> On Friday evening, July 3rd, 1868, we left home and Nashville on the Decatur train, with the view of seeing Memphis. At daylight, July 4th, we looked out upon the town of Athens, Ala., and we were perplexed at not seeing the old familiar houses, which were standing in our youth. The god of war had visited the place and had mutilated its fair proportions...Tolbert Fanning.[188]

A. J. Rollings wrote:

The Church of Christ in Athens came next, and this was around 1890. As early as 1860 preachers of the Church of Christ preached in Athens at the courthouse and other places, and a group met in private homes prior to the erection of the present meeting house. Gradually the work began to grow, and as time has passed, growth has been more rapid.[189]

Rollings made the statement about preaching in Athens during the 1860's but there is no documentation from which to draw this conclusion, however the Christian Church also makes the same claim. Whether this statement is true or not does not detract from the fact that the church was established a few years before 1890. The following reports will bear this out.

The earliest *Gospel Advocate* report came from Brown Godwin, a former Mars Hill College student. It was published in the *Gospel Advocate*:

> B. C. Goodwin, Elkmont, Ala., July 13, writes; I visited Reunion on the first Lord's day in this month and there were two added to the army of the Lord, The church is in good working order there. I expect to hold them a meeting on the first Lord's day in October. Tell Bro. Barnes to send an appointment to Athens, Ala.[190]

Here we find Goodwin making an appeal to J. M. Barnes, on behalf of the town of Athens to have a preacher sent there. Some of the Disciples' records in Athens show that A. C. Henry came to Athens to work in 1884. Apparently, Barnes had persuaded Henry to come to Athens. Barnes and Henry knew one another from their interactions in South Alabama. Somewhere between Goodwin's appeal and the end of 1884, a congregation was established. In 1894 O. P. Spiegel made his appearance in Athens. His arrival in Athens brought the first seeds of the missionary society and the use of instrumental music in worship. Spiegel was a full-fledged Disciple minister. Within six years the church in Athens would be divided. Spiegel wrote a brief report:

> Athens, July 2. Our meeting began here yesterday. At night, the house was full. Fine attention and good prospects for a fine meeting. O. P. Spiegel.[191]

Spiegel came with the intention to convert the church in Athens into a society church. An example of the intentions of the society across northern Alabama is revealed by Justus McDuffie (J. M.) Barnes in a rather lengthy article J. M. Barnes a south Alabamian and one of the writers for the *Gospel Advocate* authored the following report on a society man trying to raise money and find "the right man" to work for the missionary society in North Alabama:

> Brother Hawkins recently spent some time at Decatur trying to locate a preacher. "He made up" about five hundred dollars, which, he says, the church will pay a preacher for half his time, if he "can get the right man." I suppose he can find other churches in easy reach of Decatur which will take the other half of "the right man's" time. He said he went to Mooresville, five miles from Decatur, and spent a few days "to see one man" who is rich and will give, he thinks, twenty-five or fifty dollars a year for State missions. At Athens, about twelve miles from Decatur, he raised thirty-five dollars in a few. hours for State missions without much effort. It occurs to me that this way of depending on a State evangelist to raise money for State missions, locate preachers, select the right man, make up money to support preachers, and address everything in general is one reason the churches are all dead or dying. I do not see that much, if anything, would be lost if they were all dead, provided the State evangelist survives. As far as I can see, he is depended on to run the whole thing, anyhow. Years ago, before there was any State evangelist or any State missions in this country, men like A. C.

Henry, Bob Gibson, Jim Curtis, John Hayes, and Tom Weatherford preached the gospel and built-up churches all over this country. The churches were prosperous in those days, notwithstanding the Gospel Advocate had a much larger circulation in this country then than it has now. Somehow, as State missions and State evangelists have increased, the circulation of the Gospel Advocate has fallen off and the churches have" died out in this country. A. C. Henry lives at Athens, and that thirty-five dollars would support him to do work that ought to be done within a few miles of that place in almost any direction he could go. Jim Curtis lives a few miles from Decatur, and that five hundred dollars would support him to preach the gospel in destitute places in all that region. Tom Weatherford lives a few miles from Athens, and he would probably baptize more people and establish more churches and live on less money than "the right man." Bob Gibson lives at Hartsell, fifteen miles from Decatur; and in the days of my boyhood, when there were flourishing churches all over this country, but no State evangelists or State missions, he was considered "the right man." John Hays lives at Mooresville, and, with proper encouragement and support, he would do good preaching and establish churches in many places around his home. What is the matter with all these men now? Under the leadership of State evangelists and State missions the churches have lost confidence both in the home preachers and in their ability to manage their own affairs. They depend on State evangelists and State missions to do everything and manage everything for them. The preachers who built up the churches have been neglected and discouraged, and some of them have helped to make bad matters worse by half-hearted participation in modified forms of organized effort. State evangelists and State missions have taught the churches to look abroad for "the right man," and when he came, he was oftener than otherwise a failure with the world and a disappointment to the church. He would nurse a sickly little pastorate on theological soothing sirup through a season of summer complaint, and then

> get a State evangelist to locate him' as the right man somewhere else, leaving sensible men of the world disgusted with the farce and the church in worse condition than he found it. On this basis the churches not only neglect and discourage home preachers, but they also fail to develop any preachers at home. If the churches will take the management of their own affairs into their own hands, worship and serve the Lord for themselves under the leadership and instruction of their own elders, develop preachers at home from among their own members by the study of the Bible and the work of the Lord, and support and encourage preachers thus developed, who live here and know the people of this country, to preach the gospel and establish churches in destitute places in their immediate vicinity, they will prosper, even if some of the members do read the Gospel Advocate. J.M. Barnes.[192]

This demonstrates what the fledgling little band had to face from the missionary society group. Barnes made it clear to the readers that the society was not helping the cause of Christ, but rather hindering it.

The house spoken above in Spiegel's report must have been the old brick house that had been converted into a house of worship as is shown in the following article under the heading—"New Church Building":

> The membership of the Christian Church in this place are now taking down their little brick church building to replace it with a handsome and commodious frame church building. They are to be congratulated on their enterprise and zeal. In removing the little brick building that has served as a house of worship for some years they remove one of the old land marks of the town. This was among of the oldest brick buildings that was ever erected in this place and was built for· an office building. At times it has been used as a printing office, a law office, and a school-house and other purposes, but some years ago it was

purchased by the members of the Christian church and the partition torn out and the building converted into a church, and they have continued to use the building until it has grown entirely too small; for their needs and they have determined to build a new church. This is indeed commendable in them and while the church is not a strong one in point of membership, yet they have some of the leading businessmen and some of the most, popular ladies in the city as members and when they set to do anything they do not stop until it is accomplished. There is some objection to their building a frame building to near the square and in fact there was ordinance a few years ago prescribing a fire limit, of three hundred feet from the public square, but what has become of this we know not.[193]

J. Waller Henry, a liberal preacher, in sympathy with Spiegel, wrote the following obituary on his mother. It was copied from a Nashville newspaper and published by the *Gospel Advocate*:

Athens, Ala., October 26. —Mrs. Henry, wife of Dr. A. C. Henry, one of the most distinguished ministers in the Christian denomination, died at the home of her husband in this place yesterday with heart failure. She had been ill for some time with typhoid fever and was thought to be almost clear of fever, and her children were off at their various places of business, when they were hurriedly summoned home, but arrived too late to see their mother alive. She was most excellent woman, with many friends. Her funeral occurred in this place this morning at nine o'clock, being conducted at the residence."[194] The loss of a good wife is the saddest of bereavements, and Brother Henry has our heartfelt sympathy in his great sorrow.[195]

A few observations are in order. A. C. Henry was living in Athens at this time. His character was more like that of T. B. Larimore; but not being supported enough to support his large family, he accepted money from the missionary society and was thought to be in sympathy with it. His wife died and her funeral was conducted at their residence, which was odd. Was there no church building at this point in time? It was unusual, to say the least. It is also odd that the *Gospel Advocate* had to pick this report up from the Nashville papers, and not by having the report sent directly by J. W. Henry. This gives a hint as to his feelings toward the *Gospel Advocate*—his action in this instance was the same as the other society sympathizers—they did not like the *Gospel Advocate*'s stand against all innovations in the Disciple churches.

An example of the work of the society work is found in the reports given to the convention meeting in 1905 in Athens:

> S. P. Spiegel, general evangelist, held eighteen meetings, preached 355 sermons, baptized 112 persons, received 105 additional accessions, collected $251.46 in the field.[196]

In the minutes of the society is recorded:

> In 1905 the state convention met at Athens with Mrs. Ida Withers Harrison as the National Christian Women's Board of Missions' representative. At this convention Mrs. Aurora Pryor McClellan of Athens, a woman of many rare attainments and virtue and to whom had come many high honors, was selected the first state president.[197]

It seems as though the convention was a deliberate move to strengthen the Disciple work in Athens. Why was the meeting not in Birmingham or Montgomery or elsewhere in some other large city? This must have worked. The following year Wilburn Derryberry wrote:

> ...At Athens, the "digressives'" have done some more "missionary" work. After a good house had been built, the organ and society work was forced in over the opposition of some of the members, and they were driven from the Lord's-day worship.

This leaves me in a tent meeting two and one-half miles from this place. We have about one dozen brethren and sisters here, who seem to be in earnest. They have a large tent in a beautiful place, well-lit and plenty of song books. The meeting began on Sunday and will continue indefinitely. W. Derryberry.[198]

The *Nashville Banner* published the following under the heading—"A Great Tent Meeting" in October 1907:

A great tent meeting is now in progress here by Elder Derryberry, of Tennessee, who is supported by six county churches of the Christian faith, who are not what the local church is called, progressionists;" but they are non-progressionists in that they do not believe in instrumental music in their churches, neither do they believe in missions, so they have decided to make a fight for their side of the question here. The pastor of the Christian Church in this place, Elder Lenox, has just resigned and gone to Pensacola to accept the pastorate of the First Church in that city, and for the present the congregation here is without a pastor; but the other sect did not ask for the church, but are using a large tent and have large congregations. The evangelist is a Tennessee man and is said to be a very powerful preacher. - Athens (Ala.) special to the "Nashville Banner."[199]

This report aroused concern at the *Gospel Advocate* and with Derryberry also. It brought forth correspondence between J. C. McQuiddy and Derryberry. Derryberry gave a lengthy report on the tent meeting:

Brother McQuiddy: In the Gospel Advocate of October 31 is a clipping from the Nashville Banner, with your comment, in regard to this meeting. I appreciate your article in that it corrects some very erroneous ideas in the Banner. But there is one mistake in your comments that I think is right to correct and might be wrong not to correct. It is this: "Here is a preacher in

Athens doing mission work; he is sent there by six Tennessee churches; he receives no support from a church in Athens." In regard to the "six Tennessee churches," the first one is to report as yet. The facts are these: I went to Athens without a special promise from any church, as far as I know. There were a few members who attended from three, and perhaps four, churches around. From these and some individuals in Athens, all told, I have received to date fifteen dollars and fifty cents. The meeting was well attended and very interesting. W. Derryberry.[200]

McQuiddy responded in the same article:

I was led by the Banner correspondent to believe that six churches were cooperating with Brother Derryberry in the work at Athens, Ala. I am glad that Brother Derryberry makes the whole truth known. The work of planting churches is very much the same throughout the whole country. Earnest, sacrificing gospel preachers have gone very much at their own charges. They preached the gospel in destitute fields. Churches sprang up as if by magic in these fields. The world-wise and rich wondered how it was done. Those who love money more than the Lord are still wondering how such great results were accomplished. The names of many of these godly preachers are unknown to the world. No eloquent funeral sermon was delivered over their remains. No long newspaper article proclaimed to the world the close of a useful and noble life. No costly monument marks the place of their burial. While their names have been forgotten, their work lives after them. The influence of a noble, consecrated life is far reaching. God can use the influence of a devout life after a man is dead. Samson accomplished more in his death than in all his life. God used the dead Elisha as well as the living. Many of the truly great men are those who have broken the soil in new fields, who have borne the privations of pioneer work without a murmur. They have preached in the open air, in schoolhouses and courthouses, and wherever and whenever an opportunity presented itself. They have labored with their own hands for a support, and because they loved souls, they have done extra work and endured many privations to preach the gospel to those in darkness and sin. With the fires of enthusiasm burning on the altars of hearts filled with truth, such men have done more to plant the Gospel in new fields than missionary societies. J. C. McQuiddy.[201]

In this article, Derryberry, a grandson of Joshua K. Speer, made it clear that he had no part in working with the missionary society, and that what he had done at Athens was on his own efforts and just a few dollars from his tent work. Derryberry had moved to Athens to stay and fight the digressives. His next report proved that he was dug in for the long haul at Athens. He made the report just two years later:

> Brother W. Derryberry, of Athens, Ala., writes: "Our work in this part of the country is prospering. I am preaching regularly at six places in this (Limestone) county. We expect to begin a tent meeting at Athens on Sunday evening, May 23 to continue for several weeks. On the first Sunday in June, Brother R. N. Moody, of Albertville, Ala., is to begin here for an indefinite time. He is an excellent gospel preacher."[202]

Derryberry was preaching for six congregations in Limestone County. He probably arranged for Moody to come to Athens to hold a tent meeting. This suggests that the conservative brethren, at that time, still had no permanent place in which to worship. A Brother Sherman Sexton of Athens gave a follow-up report on that meeting, and it was published in the *Gospel Advocate*:

> Brother Sherman Sexton, R. F. D. No. 1, Athens, Ala., writes, under date of May 24: "Brother W. Derryberry began a mission meeting in Athens last night. Brother R. N. Moody, of Albertville, Ala., will be here on the first Lord's day in June to

continue the meeting indefinitely. I will preach at Brown's Chapel, Maury County, Tenn., on the second Sunday in June."
[203]

Following this report, someone at the *Gospel Advocate* office made another report on the same tent meeting:

Brother W. Derryberry, of Athens, Ala., gave this office a pleasant visit last Monday. For two weeks he has been engaged in tent meetings in Athens. Brother R. N. Moody, of Albertville, Ala., has taken up the work there, and will continue the meetings indefinitely.[204]

In August Derryberry and a friend—a Brother Farrar preached in a cotton factory in Athens, which suggests that the brethren had no house of their own at that time. Author of that report is unknown but was published in the *Gospel Advocate*:

Brethren W. Derryberry and Farrar recently closed a meeting at the cotton factory, Athens, Ala., with three baptized. Brother Derryberry is now in a meeting at a Methodist meetinghouse six miles east of Athens, preaching to large audiences.[205]

In 1910 F. C. Sowell, another former Mars Hill student, came to Athens and held a meeting. He had the following to say about the work among the faithful brethren:

Columbia, August 5. I began a meeting at Brown's Chapel, Maury County, on the third Lord's day in July and continued it till Friday, with growing interest. Then Brother John Rainey continued it till Sunday night, baptizing one and restoring one. On Saturday before the fourth Lord's day in July I went to Athens, Ala., and was met by Brother Wilburn Derryberry, who had made some appointments for me. I preached at Corinth Church, seven miles from town, at eleven o'clock, at a schoolhouse at three o'clock in the afternoon, and at Athens at night. We have a faithful little band in Athens. On Monday I went fifteen miles in the Country and preached (sic) seven days where we have a small band of brethren. We had fine crowds and two were baptized. The people in that part of the country are mostly Methodists and Baptists, but they came out to the meetings well. Much preaching is needed in this part of North Alabama. F. C. Sowell.[206]

Sowell refers to the conservative group as "a small band of brethren." The church was still struggling numerically, but strong in faith and determination. Derryberry gave another report on the work in or near Athens. Unfortunately, we do not know which. He just refers to it as a new work. I give the *Gospel Advocate* report:

> Brother W. Derryberry writes from Athens, Ala.: "The meeting with the new congregation planted a year ago began last Sunday. Large crowds in attendance. The interest is good, but no additions so far. The meeting will continue over next Lord's day. We hope for good results."[207]

As early as 1904, Derryberry and the work at Athens had become an example of staying with a mission field. He continued for some years entrenched in Limestone County and the Athens area. L. C. Chisholm, a native of Tuscumbia, Alabama wrote the following after T. W. Phillips came to East Alabama and held a very good meeting. Chisholm was making an appeal for Phillips to be located in East Alabama and North Georgia and do mission work. We give a part of the appeal as published in the journal *Firm Foundation*:

> ...If he would begin here as a brother has begun at Athens, Ala., and Brother Fuqua at Florence and Brother Fonner at Cullman, Ala., and stick to this work in a few years great results would

grow out of the labors in Alabama. We trust Brother Phillips will duly consider this matter. L. C. Chisholm.[208]

Sowell's report, dated August 22, 1912 (956) was the last *Gospel Advocate* article to mention the Athens church before 1914. Thus, with the above reports, we close our study on the church in Athens.

Union Grove

A work was attempted at a place called "Union Grove" in Limestone County. T. L. Weatherford and J. R. Bradley both preached in meetings at this place. J. R. Bradley had just closed a successful meeting at Maplewood in southern Giles County, Tennessee in August, seven days earlier. His next meeting was at Union Grove, Limestone County, Alabama. We do not know exactly what J.R. did the week following Maplewood because his meeting at Union Grove began seven days afterward. We do not know if he traveled home for a few days or if, perhaps, he visited with old friends. Brother T.L. Weatherford did live in the area and he and J.R. had been friends since their Mars Hill days. This meeting ran from August 30th through September 4th (the first Friday).

Bradley was the first one to make mention of the work at Union Grove in the *Gospel Advocate*. The report was a part of a lengthy article on Bradley's work for the year 1896. A few lines revealed this work:

> ... On the fifth Sunday in August we began at Union Grove, Limestone County, Ala., and closed on Friday night following

with four confessions and baptisms, and one from the Methodist body ... J. R. Bradley.[209]

With no comment on where this place was located, we have no way of knowing just where this took place. Another meeting was held in 1897 and was reported jointly by T. L. Weatherford and J. R. Bradley. This report contained more information on Union Grove. We give it as follows:

> Aug. 31. Our meeting at Union Grove, Limestone County, Ala., which began the fourth Sunday in this month, closed the fifth Sunday, with nine confessions and baptisms and one restored. This also was a meeting where all the preaching was done in the daytime, with dinner on the ground. Such work, we believe, is better for both preachers and audience. On this trip forty-two from all sources have been added to the congregations. Our work together in this field has been very pleasant to us and, we hope, profitable to the cause. J. R. Bradley and T. L. Weatherford.[210]

These two reports are all the information contained in the *Gospel Advocate* in relation to this Union Grove. What became of this work? J. D. Jones mentioned a meeting at a location called "Union Schoolhouse "on Florence Road. His statement is given here:

> ... On the 3rd Lord's day in August I began a meeting at Pleasant Point. On Wednesday, the meeting was moved to Union Schoolhouse, on the Florence road. and continued till Friday night. Four persons were baptised during the meeting ... .[211]

Could "Union Schoolhouse" be connected to the Union Grove work? What is more confusing about the Union Grove work is the fact that A. J. Rollings never mentioned it in his history of the Churches of Christ in Limestone County.

Perhaps this work merged with another congregation before Rollings' wrote his history or it never became an established work. If so, what became of those people who were baptized by Weatherford and Bradley? There was a total of forty-six baptized in the two meetings reported. There is one possibility—it could have merged with Pleasant Point since they were close enough that the meeting was moved from Pleasant Point to Union Schoolhouse. [212] Maybe someone in the future can solve this mystery. We now look at other places in Limestone County.

Cartwright

There were Christians living at Cartwright long before there was a congregation at that place, The J. W. Myers family lived there,[213] as well as M. E. Terry and family.[214]

In August 1911 J. Petty Ezell reported, probably, the first effort to establish a work at Cartwright:

> Brother J. P. Ezell is in a mission meeting at Cartwright, Ala., under a brush arbor. His meeting at Oakland, nine miles from Athens Ala., closed with ten baptized, four restored, and one from the Baptists.[215]

Later in the month, Ezell made a second report. He wrote from Cartwright, Ala., on August 24, 1911, saying:

> "I began a meeting at this place on Monday. August 14, and closed it last night. Although the gospel is almost nineteen centuries old, it was perfectly new to this section. Seven were baptized into Christ and many others were fully convinced. but did not have sufficient courage to obey. Brother J. P. Jones, my father in the gospel was with us two nights. We hope to build a meetinghouse here soon."[216]

Ezell relates to the reader that his father in the gospel [the one who converted him] was J. P. Jones and that this was a new work at Cartwright. He also pointed out that the Christians there desired to build a house of worship at Cartwright. This short sketch is all of the information found in the *Gospel Advocate*.

Oakland

T. C. Little gave the first report on the work at Oakland. It was full of information for those of us who are interested in historical facts. He stated:

> Began preaching at Oakland, Ala., third Lord's day in October, and continued until Tuesday night. Spoke six times to small audiences, without any additions to the church. The weather, prejudices, and gathering of. crops all were unfavorable for a meeting; yet we left feeling that some were almost persuaded to obey the Lord. May they be spared to do so yet. The little band at Oakland numbers only thirteen; yet we do not think we ever saw a better nucleus for a church. They meet every first day of the week, and worship God according to the Devine directory, and are earnest, zealous Christians during the week. Only one or two in the congregation, of whom the above cannot be truthfully said. Our visit was very pleasant by the kindness of the brothers and sisters. Bro. A—; insists that the meeting was a success. T. C. Little.[217]

Little returned in November 1884 and held another meeting. The report was an abbreviated report. It read:

T. C. Little, Fayetteville, Tenn., November 6, writes: "Returned home from a trip to Oakland, Alabama, Tuesday. No additions. [218]

Little returned for a third consecutive meeting in August 1885. He gave a report of four baptisms and one placing membership. It reads:

> The meeting at Oakland, Ala., closed last Sunday night with a large and attentive audience. Meeting continued eight days and nights with four additions by baptism, and one by commendation. The congregations were larger than usual. It was thought to be the best meeting we have ever had in that section. The little band that has been struggling so long and hard to maintain the cause here, seem encouraged and inspired with renewed energy. I can never forget their many kindnesses, earnest cooperation. with the preacher. T. C. Little.[219]

Our next report came over twenty years later. This time Wilburn Derryberry held a meeting at the Oakland congregation. Derryberry gave a good picture of the work at Oakland in the following report:

> Kenton, August 1. Our meeting at Oakland, Ala., began on the third Lord's day in July and closed at the water on Wednesday after the fourth Lord's day. This was certainly a very enjoyable meeting. It was begun by Brother Frank Morrow, of Mount Pleasant, Tenn., and had grown to be very interesting when I reached there on Wednesday. There were large crowds, especially at night, notwithstanding much rain. There are some kind-hearted brethren and sisters at that place. This is the home of two good preachers-Brother Thomas L. Weatherford, who has almost worn his life away preaching the gospel, while to a good degree supporting himself by hard labor, and Brother J. D. Jones. Three were baptized and one wanderer was

restored. We find a great deal of work to be done in North Alabama. Brother Morrow and I expect to return there the first of September and do some more work... W. Derryberry. [220]

Two years afterward, Derryberry returned and held another meeting in which, within two days, two souls were rescued from the clutches of the devil. The report follows:

Athens, July 28.-The meeting at Brymer's Schoolhouse, in Maury County, Tenn., began on the third Sunday in this month. I preached till Thursday night following—large and very attentive audiences, but there were no additions. I left the meeting with Brethren Morrow and Murphy, to be continued till Sunday night. I am now in a meeting with the Oakland Church, nine miles west from Athens. We are having very large crowds, and at this writing, with the meeting two days old, there have been two additions. I think the prospects are very bright for a good meeting. This is near the old home of Brother Weatherford, who passed away last April, after having labored in this county for thirty-five years. W. Derryberry. [221]

Derryberry gave a follow-up report on the above meeting as follows:

Culleoka, Aug. 17.-The meeting at Oakland, Ala., began on the fourth Lord's day in July and continued until the following Friday night. We had large crowds and good interest throughout. There were five baptized, one from the Methodists, one from the Baptists, and two restored. There are some good brothers and sisters at this place, and it is a pleasure to work for them. Like many others, the meeting was too short, and so we may have another in October. The work in Limestone County has been sadly neglected and there is much to be done. Many people seem willing to listen to the truth, and I am sure that with earnest, faithful work, great results will be seen in the next few years. W. Derryberry.[222]

He also gave other pertinent information such as the spiritual condition of Limestone County. No wonder Rollings could only count six established congregations in Limestone County before 1900. In 1909 J. T. Harris appeared on the scene at Oakland. He would preach the next two meetings, but there were three different reports in the *Gospel Advocate* concerning Oakland. The first report:

> Brother J. T. Harris recently closed a meeting at Bethel, Limestone County, Ala., with eleven baptized and three restored. On August 18 he closed a meeting at Oakland, nine miles from Athens, Ala., with twenty baptized, six restored, two from the Baptists, and one from the Methodists who had already been immersed. He is now in a meeting at Greenwood, Giles County, Tenn.[223]

During this first meeting, he baptized 11 and had three restorations. Below are the two reports on his second meeting at Oakland:

> Brother J. T. Harris writes from Athens, Ala., under date of August 1: "I am In a very interesting meeting at Oakland, Limestone County, Ala., with eight baptized and two restored to date. The meeting will continue for the greater part of this week. My next meeting will be at Bethel, a few miles east of this place." [224]

Harris' follow-up report was on the same page as his report on the August 1910 meeting:

> Brother J. T. Harris, of Florence, Ala., is in a meeting at Bethel, six miles east of Athens, Ala. He recently closed a meeting at

Oakland, near Athens, with ten baptized, four restored, and one from the Baptists.[225]

Two weeks later Wilburn Derryberry spoke of Harris' meeting at Oakland in his report on the Limestone County work.[226] With this report comes the end of information on Oakland, as found in the *Gospel Advocate*. This stops us four years before our overall cutoff date of 1914.

Holland's Gin

The first mention of Holland's Gin was published in an announcement of an intended meeting by J. R. Bradley in the August 7th issue of the *Gospel Advocate*, and repeated September 11th. It was his schedule for the last half of the year 1913. We give his schedule as follows:

> Kelso, Tenn., July 28.-I will begin a meeting at Elkwood, Ala., on the third Sunday In August; at old Sharon, Ala., the first Sunday in September; at Reunion, Ala., the third Sunday in September; at Holland's Gin, the first Sunday in October; and at the Elk Cotton Mills, Fayetteville, Tenn., the fourth Sunday In October. These are all the meetings I have promised. Pray for us. J. R. Bradley.[227]

From Reunion, he traveled to Holland's Gin and conducted a brush arbor meeting. The meeting began on the first Sunday in October. He never reported the results from Holland's Gin.[228]

Bradley's effort was clearly the first effort of this kind in Holland's Gin area. Unfortunately, he never reported the results of that meeting.

To restore a partial history of Holland's Gin, we must go

beyond our set boundaries of time—1914. William Thomas Goalen, an immigrant preacher from Northwest England, came to Holland's Gin and held a tent meeting. He wrote of this:

> Veto, September 19.-The work in this part of Limestone County is progressing slowly, but surely. I used the Lynnville and Pulaski tent at Holland's Gin for two weeks, with four additions to the one body, and got a band of disciples there to meet at their homes and keep house for the Lord...W. T. Goalen.[229]

Goalen's visit brought the church nearer to a sound work and in the next report, five years later, helped set the small band on the right path. It was reported by H. F. Williams in 1921:

> We can but admire the faith and zeal of a brother who reports that he is "picking cotton through the week and preaching the gospel on Lord's days." Here is such a report from William W. Still of Athens, Ala.: "I am here in my old home in Northern Alabama, picking cotton through the week and preaching the gospel on Lord's days. On the third Lord's day in this month, I preached in Brother Biggerstaff's home. We have ten brethren near Holland's Gin. just four of these brethren meet on Lord's day. These four brethren meet in each other's homes to break bread. On the first Lord's day in November, I will preach in my old home church-Reunion. I will do evangelistic work here in January and will then return to the Burritt Bible College in Spencer, Tenn." H. F. Williams.[230]

With Williams' report, we leave Holland's Gin behind to be dealt with by some later history student.

CORINTH

One other congregation must be mentioned from this period—Corinth. Little can be gleaned from the journals of that period. We do not know the exact date of its establishment, but we know it was established by 1910.[231] If we follow an undocumented statement in the history of the Corinth/Jones Road Congregation, it would be as early as 1908, or earlier.

The first *Gospel Advocate* report was made by W. Derryberry. It read as follows:

> Athens, August 18. Brother F. C. Sowell, of Columbia, Tenn., recently held a meeting of eight-days' duration at Mechanic's Chapel, in this county, with two baptized. Brother J. T. Harris, of Florence, recently held a meeting at Oakland, with ten baptized and four restored; and one at Bethel, with four baptized and one restored. He is now in a meeting at Corinth, with good crowds. The brethren speak well of the work of these preachers. Brother L. Hodson and I lately held a meeting of eight days duration with the New Hope Church, which, on account of troubles within, had ceased to meet. We had good interest, and the brethren agreed to go to work again. Wilburn Derryberry. [232]

The last report we use is found in the *Gospel Advocate* of November 9, 1916, which takes us two years beyond our time parameter of 1914. It was a report on gospel meetings held for the summer and fall of 1916 by J. T. Clark:

> Pulaski, October 30.-The following is a brief report on my summer and fall protracted-meeting work: Cherry Creek, White County, Tenn., beginning on July 16, thirteen days, seven baptisms, one from the Baptists, five restorations; Reunion, Limestone County, Ala., July 30, six days, two baptisms, one restoration; Hayes' Mill, Ala., August 6, tent meeting, twelve days, three baptisms, four restorations; Corinth, Limestone County, August 20, nine days, eight baptisms, six restorations; Bethel, Limestone County, September 8, eight days, four baptisms, two restorations; Ephesus (new church), September 17, ten days, eighteen baptisms, thirteen restorations... J. T. Clark.[233]

The published history of the congregation gives us the only other information we have discovered. It is a compact history and reads as follows:

> The church of Christ on Jones Road was formerly named the Corinth church of Christ. The name was changed in 2008 when the congregation moved into a new facility on Jones Road—Jones Road Building. The Corinth church started in 1908 in the Old Johnson school. This schoolhouse was located at the corner of Nick Davis Road and McCulley Mill Road in the eastern part of Limestone County in North Alabama. The building is believed to have been built in 1912. Land was donated by John Pepper and J.C. Bailey. Construction was of wood siding with a tin roof. Inside, there were wooden slatted pews, gas lanterns, and a wood stove for heat. There was not a regular preacher. When a preacher would visit, the youngsters loved to sit on the floor in a semicircle in front of the pulpit.

In these early days, the church met only on Sunday mornings for about an hour of singing, praying, reading, classes, and the Lord's Supper. The communion table was covered with two white starched cloths; one to cover the table and the second to cover the emblems. The fruit of the vine was contained in two glasses. These were passed around for each member to partake. The bread was placed on glass plates and passed around.[234]

With this scanty information, we draw our conclusions and give this short history of Corinth and close our history of the Restoration Movement in Limestone County. We hope someone in the future can add a more detailed history of Corinth.

Endnotes

[1] Asa Monroe Plyler, *Historical Sketches of the Churches of Christ in Alabama, 1940's* (Henderson, TN: Hester Publications), 17.

[2] Loretta Merrell Ekis, Official Limestone County website, History of Limestone County.

[3] Plyler, *Historical Sketches of the Churches of Christ in Alabama, 1940's*, 19; A.J. Rollings, *Limestone Democrat* (March 1939), unknown.

[4] *Christian Reformer* (August 1829), 379.

[5] Geoge H. Watson, and Mildred B. Watson, *History of the Christian Churches in the Alabama Area* (St. Louis, MO: The Bethany Press, 1965), 157.

[6] Andrew B. Ellis, *The Effect of the Restoration Movement of America on Limestone County, Alabama Prior to the Civil War* (December 15, 2000), https://drewellisfamily.tripod.com/restmov1.htm.

[7] *Christian Messenger* (November 1827), 17–18.

[8] *Christian Messenger* (November 1827), 17–18.

[9] *Bible Advocate* (October 1, 1848), 186.

[10] *Christian Messenger* (April 1829), 142.

[11] *Christian Messenger* (December 1829), 16–17.

[12] *Christian Messenger* (December 1830), 284–285.

[13] *Christian Messenger* (January 1832), 26–27.
[14] *Christian Messenger* (March 1832), 94.
[15] *Christian Messenger* (December 1832), 276.
[16] *Christian Messenger* (September 1833), 287.
[17] *Christian Messenger* (September 1833), 279.
[18] *Gospel Advocate* (October 12, 1898), 649.
[19] *Christian Reformer* (December 1844), 287.
[20] *Christian Journal* (November 1845), 237; *Christian Reformer* (December 1845), 287.
[21] *Messenger and Advocate* (June 1847), 139. The *Bible Advocate* had merged with the *Christian Messenger* and was addressed as the *Messenger and Advocate* thereafter).
[22] *Bible Advocate* (J. H. Dunn. White Sulphur Spring, Ala., August 21, 1848).
[23] J. H. Grime, *History of Middle Tennessee Baptists* (Nashville, TN: Baptist and Reflector, 1902), 539.
[24] Grime, *History of Middle Tennessee Baptists*, 539–540.
[25] This is taken from the names of the defectors found in the pages of Grime's book.
[26] Hosea Holcombe, *A History of the Rise and Progress of the Baptists in Alabama* (Philadelphia: King and Baird, 1840), 279.
[27] Federal Land Certificate (April 7, 1818), No. 277.
[28] Bobby Graham, *The Alabama Restoration Journal* (October 1, 2011), 9–10).
[29] Graham, 9–10.
[30] *Christian Baptist* (March 3, 1828), 200.
[31] *Christian Baptist* (July 6, 1829), 302.
[32] *Christian Baptist* (December 5, 1829), 130.
[33] *Minutes of the Duck River Association of Baptists* (Shelbyville, TN: John Newton Printer), 2.
[34] *Millennial Harbinger* (January 1834), 45.
[35] *Evangelist* (September 1, 1834), 216.
[36] *Evangelist* (December 3, 1834), 282.
[37] *Millennial Harbinger* (January 1835), 38.
[38] Graham, 9.

[39] From PowerPoint Lesson by Bobby Graham—Athens Post, September 1869.

[40] Maud Biard Smith, "Biard Family History," (n.d.), 31.

[41] (J. S.(H). Hundley, "Letters," *The Evangelist* (May 1, 1840), 113). The name was misprinted. It should have been J. H. Hundley.

[42] Carroll Kendrick, "No Title," *The Christian Preacher* (November 1839), 218–219; J. S. (J. H.) Hundley, "Letters," *The Evangelist* (May 1, 1840), 113.

[43] Tolbert Fanning, "Notes On Tour," *Christian Review* (November 1844), 243.

[44] Tolbert Fanning, "Notes On Tour," *Christian Review* (November 1844), 243.

[45] *Gospel Advocate* (April 14, 1886), 236.

[46] Tolbert Fanning, "Notes On Tour," *Christian Review* (November 1844), 243.

[47] J. H. Dunn, "A Call For Preachers And Teachers," *Christian Magazine* (September 1849), 350.

[48] J. H. Dunn, "A Call For Preachers And Teachers," *Christian Magazine* (September 1849), 350.

[49] J. J. Trott, "Report on Evangelists, *Christian Magazine* (August 1851), 253.

[50] J. J. Trott, "Report on Evangelists—No. 8," *Christian Magazine*, (January 1852), 29.

[51] J. H. Dunn, "Alabama," *Millennial Harbinger* (April 1853), 235.

[52] "Church of Christ at Mooresville," A Historical Tract (No Date).

[53] J. H. Dunn, *Gospel Advocate* (January 1857), 24.

[54] "Church of Christ at Mooresville," A Historical Tract (No Date).

[55] Tolbert Fanning, "A Month's Tour," *Gospel Advocate* (January 1858), 3.

[56] Tolbert Fanning, "A Month's Tour," *Gospel Advocate* (January 1858), 3.

[57] Tolbert Fanning, "The Plan of Salvation," *Gospel Advocate* (March 1858), 87–88.

[58] O. P. Miller, "No Title," *Gospel Advocate* (August 1860), 254.

[59] Tolbert Fanning, "Visit To North Alabama," *Gospel Advocate* (November 1860), 343–344.

[60] "Obituary Notices," *Millennial Harbinger* (February 1861), 120.

[61] James A. Garfield, "Letter To Mrs. James A. Garfield," Garfield Papers: Manuscript Division, Library of Congress, Washington DC (July 5, 1863).

[62] J. M. Pickens, *Gospel Advocate* (October 20, 1868), 1044. Bro. J. M. Pickens's name in our absence was printed J. W. Pickings, in a call for a meeting at Mooresville, Ala. *Gospel Advocate* (November 12, 1868), 1088.

[63] *Gospel Advocate* (April 11, 1867), 296.

[64] *Gospel Advocate* (July 5, 1877), 422.

[65] *Gospel Advocate* (July 15, 1880), 461.

[66] *Christian Standard* (October 27, 1888), 683.

[67] Department of Commerce and Labor, Bureau of the Census, *Religious Bodies: 1906* (Washington: Government Printing Office, 1910): 1.294.

[68] Plyler, *Historical Sketches of the Churches of Christ in Alabama*, 18–19.

[69] *Christian Review* (November 1844), 243.

[70] *Gospel Advocate* (November 1860), 343–344.

[71] *Gospel Advocate* (December 1860), 370.

[72] *Gospel Advocate* (September 19, 1867), 758–759.

[73] *Gospel Advocate* (September 26, 1867), 775.

[74] *Gospel Advocate* (September 1, 1870), 801.

[75] *Gospel Advocate* (October 27, 1870), 990.

[76] *Gospel Advocate* (October 19, 1871), 975.

[77] *Gospel Advocate* (September 18, 1879), 603.

[78] *Gospel Advocate* (October 2, 1879), 633.

[79] *Gospel Advocate* (August 19, 1880), 541.

[80] *The Alabama Courier*, Athens, Alabama, (March 31, 1881), 3.
[81] *Gospel Advocate* (October 29, 1881), 662.
[82] *Gospel Advocate* (May 11, 1882), 294.
[83] *Gospel Advocate* (July 23, 1884), 475.
[84] *Gospel Advocate* (October 21, 1891), 665.
[85] *Gospel Advocate* (Aug. 20, 1896), 540–541.
[86] *Gospel Advocate* (September 27, 1906), 618.
[87] *Gospel Advocate* (October 4, 1906), 637.
[88] *Gospel Advocate* (August 22, 1907), 533.
[89] *Gospel Advocate* (August 6, 1908), 501.
[90] *Gospel Advocate* (August 26, 1909), 1072.
[91] *Gospel Advocate* (August 26, 1909), 1077.
[92] *Gospel Advocate* (February 17, 1910), 214–215.
[93] *Gospel Advocate* (November 3, 1910), 213.
[94] *Gospel Advocate* (November 10, 1910), 241.
[95] *Gospel Advocate* (August 24, 1911), 948.
[96] *Gospel Advocate* (September 7, 1911), 1009.
[97] *Gospel Advocate* (August 7, 1912), 756.
[98] *Gospel Advocate* (October 24, 1912), 1173.
[99] *Gospel Advocate* (October 16, 1913), 997.
[100] *Gospel Advocate* (October 22, 1914), 1108.
[101] *Gospel Advocate* (August 26, 1897), 541.
[102] Plyler, *Historical Sketches of the Churches of Christ in Alabama*, 17–24.
[103] Plyler, *Historical Sketches of the Churches of Christ in Alabama*, 20–21.
[104] *Gospel Advocate* (October 3, 1867), 800.
[105] *Gospel Advocate* (October 25, 1877), 660.
[106] *Gospel Advocate* (September 14, 1871), 850.
[107] *Gospel Advocate* (August 26, 1897), 541.
[108] *Gospel Advocate* (September 10, 1874), 852.
[109] *Gospel Advocate* (August 25, 1892), 540.
[110] *Gospel Advocate* (October 7, 1875), 958.
[111] *Gospel Advocate* (November 4, 1875), 1056.

[112] *Gospel Advocate* (September 7, 1876), 876.
[113] *Gospel Advocate* (October 26, 1876), 1045.
[114] *Gospel Advocate* (July. 19, 1877), 443.
[115] *Gospel Advocate* (October 2, 1879), 633.
[116] *Gospel Advocate* (July 1, 1880), 423.
[117] *Gospel Advocate* (September 9, 1880), 589.
[118] *Gospel Advocate* (December I. 1881), 758.
[119] *Gospel Advocate* (October 22, 1884), 84.
[120] *Gospel Advocate* (September 26, 1888), 3.
[121] *Gospel Advocate* (January 30, 1889), 79.
[122] *Gospel Advocate* (September 11, 1889), 579.
[123] *Gospel Advocate* (December 3, 1891), 765.
[124] *Gospel Advocate* (August 25, 1892), 540.
[125] *Gospel Advocate* (September 1, 1892), 556.
[126] *Gospel Advocate* (October 13, 1892), 652.
[127] *Gospel Advocate* (October 13, 1892), 652.
[128] *Gospel Advocate* (August 24, 1893), 533.
[129] *Gospel Advocate* (August 31, 1893), 556.
[130] *Gospel Advocate* (September 14, 1893), 595.
[131] *Gospel Advocate* (September 5, 1895), 572.
[132] *Gospel Advocate* (February 13, 1896), 109.
[133] *Gospel Advocate* (August 13, 1896), 525.
[134] *Gospel Advocate* (August 20, 1896), 540–541.
[135] *Gospel Advocate* (October 8, 1896), 653.
[136] *Gospel Advocate* (August 26, 1897), 541.
[137] *Gospel Advocate* (September 24, 1903), 620.
[138] *Gospel Advocate* (October 7, 1920), 976.
[139] Plyler, *Historical Sketches of the Churches of Christ in Alabama*, 17.
[140] *Gospel Advocate* (October 23, 1879), 683.
[141] *Gospel Advocate* (September 5, 1883), 568.
[142] *Gospel Advocate* (October 23, 1879), 683.
[143] *Gospel Advocate* (July 21, 1886), 459.
[144] *Gospel Advocate* (December 26, 1883), 823.
[145] *Gospel Advocate* (July 21, 1886), 459.

[146] *Gospel Advocate* (January 19, 1887), 43.
[147] *Gospel Advocate* (March 2, 1887), 139.
[148] *Gospel Advocate* (September 28, 1887), 610.
[149] *Gospel Advocate* (September 23, 1891), 601.
[150] *Gospel Advocate* (November 2, 1893), 700.
[151] *Gospel Advocate* (October 12, 1893), 652.
[152] *Gospel Advocate* (September. 26, 1895), 620.
[153] *Gospel Advocate* (October 3, 1895), 636.
[154] *Gospel Advocate* (November 18, 1897), 736.
[155] *Gospel Advocate* (September 15, 1910), 1044.
[156] *Gospel Advocate* (August 15, 1912), 932.
[157] *Gospel Advocate* (August 14, 1913), 780.
[158] *Gospel Advocate* (August 27, 1914), 918.
[159] *Gospel Advocate* (August 27, 1914), 918.
[160] *Gospel Advocate* (December 17, 1914), 1338.
[161] *Gospel Advocate* (June 8, 1916), 565.
[162] Bethel's History, from a directory, 3.
[163] Plyler, *Historical Sketches of the Churches of Christ in Alabama*, 19.
[164] *Gospel Advocate* (September 23, 1885), 599.
[165] *Gospel Advocate* (September 29, 1886), 622.
[166] *Gospel Advocate* (January 19, 1887), 43.
[167] *Gospel Advocate* (JMarch 9, 1887), 155.
[168] *Gospel Advocate* (JMarch 9, 1887), 155.
[169] *Gospel Advocate* (JMarch 9, 1887), 155.
[170] *Gospel Advocate* (August 31, 1887), 554.
[171] *Gospel Advocate* (May 22, 1889), 330.
[172] *Gospel Advocate* (August 13, 1890), 520.
[173] *Gospel Advocate* (September 2, 1891), 552.
[174] *Gospel Advocate* (September 9, 1891), 565.
[175] *Gospel Advocate* (September 1, 1892), 556.
[176] *Gospel Advocate* (September 29, 1892), 620.
[177] *Gospel Advocate* (September 14, 1893), 595.
[178] *Gospel Advocate* (September 28, 1893), 620.
[179] *Gospel Advocate* (September 5, 1895), 672.

[180] *Gospel Advocate* (October 3, 1895), 632.
[181] *Gospel Advocate* (September 24, 1896), 621.
[182] *Gospel Advocate* (February 17, 1898), 112.
[183] *Gospel Advocate* (September 28, 1899), 620.
[184] *Gospel Advocate* (August 12, 1909). 1013.
[185] *Gospel Advocate* (August 26, 1909), 1073.
[186] *Gospel Advocate* (August 12, 1909), 1013.
[187] *Gospel Advocate* (August 24, 1911), 948.
[188] *Gospel Advocate* (August 13, 1868), 774.
[189] A. J. Rollings, *Athens Courier* (March 1939). Plyler, *Historical Sketches of the Churches of Christ in Alabama*, 21.
[190] *Gospel Advocate* (July 23, 1884), 475.
[191] *Gospel Advocate* (July 12, 1894), 438.
[192] *Gospel Advocate* (June 1, 1899), front page.
[193] *Athens Courier* (November 1, 1900).
[194] *Nashville American* (October 27, 1899).
[195] *Gospel Advocate* (November 2, 1899), 693.
[196] *Disciples of Christ Minutes of American Christian Missionary Society*—1905.
[197] *Disciples of Christ Minutes of American Christian Missionary Society*—1905.
[198] *Gospel Advocate* (August 9, 1906), 50.
[199] *Gospel Advocate* (October 31, 1907), 692.
[200] *Gospel Advocate* (November 28. 1907), 756.
[201] *Gospel Advocate* (November 28. 1907), 756.
[202] *Gospel Advocate* (May 27, 1909), 657.
[203] *Gospel Advocate* (June 3, 1909), 688.
[204] *Gospel Advocate* (June 10, 1909), 720.
[205] *Gospel Advocate* (August 26, 1909), 1072.
[206] *Gospel Advocate* (September 1, 1910), 1001.
[207] *Gospel Advocate* (August 22, 1912), 956.
[208] *Firm Foundation* (May 24, 1904), 5.
[209] *Gospel Advocate* (September 24, 1896), 621.
[210] *Gospel Advocate* (September 9, 1897), 573.
[211] *Gospel Advocate* (September 24, 1903), 620.

[212] *Gospel Advocate* (September 24, 1903), 620.
[213] *Gospel Advocate* (January 30, 1889), 79.
[214] *Gospel Advocate* (August 25, 1892), 540.
[215] *Gospel Advocate* (August 24, 1911), 944.
[216] *Gospel Advocate* (August 31, 1911), 977.
[217] *Gospel Advocate* (October 31, 1883), 694.
[218] *Gospel Advocate* (November 19, 1884), 743.
[219] *Gospel Advocate* (August 29, 1885), 543.
[220] *Gospel Advocate* (August 9, 1906), 509.
[221] *Gospel Advocate* (August 6, 1908), 508.
[222] *Gospel Advocate* (August 27, 1908), 559.
[223] *Gospel Advocate* (August 26, 1909), 1073.
[224] *Gospel Advocate* (August 18, 1910), 948.
[225] *Gospel Advocate* (August 18, 1910), 948.
[226] *Gospel Advocate* (September 1, 1910), 1000.
[227] *Gospel Advocate* (August 7, 1913), 756; (Sept. 11, 1913), 877.
[228] *Gospel Advocate* (Oct. 9, 1913), 973.
[229] *Gospel Advocate* (September 28, 1916), 974.
[230] *Gospel Advocate* (November 3, 1921), 1076.
[231] *Gospel Advocate* (September 1, 1910), 1000.
[232] *Gospel Advocate* (September 1, 1910), 1000.
[233] *Gospel Advocate* (November 9, 1916), 1119.
[234] Jones Road Church of Christ History http://www.jonesroadchurch.org/about/congregation-history.

Bibliography

Books

Grime, J. H. *History of Middle Tennessee Baptists*. Nashville, TN: Baptist and Reflector, 1902.

Holcombe, Hosea. *A History of the Rise and Progress of the Baptists in Alabama*. Philadelphia, PA: King and Baird, 1840.

Plyler, Asa Monroe. *Historical Sketches of the Churches of Christ in Alabama, 1940's*. Henderson, TN: Hester Publications, n.d.

Watson, Geoge H., and Mildred B. Watson, *History of the Christian Churches in the Alabama Area*. St. Louis, MO: The Bethany Press, 1965.

Periodicals

Alabama Christian
The Alabama Courier
The Alabama Restoration Journal
Athens Courier
Bible Advocate
Christian Baptist
Christian Journal
Christian Magazine
Christian Messenger
The Christian Preacher
Christian Reformer
Christian Review
Christian Standard
Evangelist
Firm Foundation
Gospel Advocate
Limestone Democrat
Messenger and Advocate
Millennial Harbinger
Nashville American

Name Index

Abernathy, H. C.   36, 61–62, 66
Anderson, James Clark   8, 18
Barnes, Justus McDuffie (J. M.)   34, 83–84, 86
Biard, John Nelson   16, 19
Bradley, J. R.   34–35, 40–43, 46, 56–58, 79–80, 95, 97, 105
Campbell, Alexander   2, 12–14, 16–17, 19
Collinsworth, James Ragin (J. R.)   5, 10
Derryberry, Wilburn (W.)   81, 88–93
Dunn, John Henry (J.H.)   5, 10–11, 18, 21–22, 27–31, 35–36, 45–49, 52, 111–112
Elley, George W.   21
Fanning, Tolbert   10, 21–23, 26–27, 36, 82, 112–113
Favor, John (Jr.)   15–19
Favor, John (Sr.)   14–15, 17–19
Godwin, Brown   83

Goodwin, B. C.   34, 80, 83
Griffith, Thacker V.   18
Henry, A. C.   83, 85, 87
Holbrook, J. H.   47
Hundley, J. H. (John Henry)   20, 22–23, 26–27, 36, 112
Jackson, W. E. (Wm.)   52
Kendrick, Allen   9–10, 45
Kendrick, Carroll   20, 22, 112
Larimore, T. B.   24, 32–33, 36, 79, 87
Lipscomb, David   24, 29–30, 36
Lipscomb, Granville   30, 36, 45
Little, T. C.   100–101
Lynn, Benjamin   2–3
Matthews, James E.   3–9
Matthews, Mansel W.   8
Morrow, Frank H.   35–37, 101–102
Morton, James (J. H.)   21, 34–36, 52–56, 77–78

Nance, Thomas G. 33–34, 51
Northcross, M. H. 37, 79–80
Officer, Robert Wallace 36, 50, 65
Pepper, Franklin 73–75, 80–81
Pickens, J. M. 24, 113
Plyler, Asa M. 1–2, 44–45, 60, 73, 110, 113–117, 119
Rollings, Adolphus Jackson (A. J.) 2, 26, 44–45, 60, 62, 67, 73–74, 82–83, 96–97, 103, 110, 117
Scott, Walter 2, 17, 20
Sowell, F. C. 92–94, 107
Speer, Joshua Kennerly (J. K., Joshua K.) 5, 10, 14, 16–18, 36, 91
Speer, W. S. 5, 10
Spiegel, Oliver Pickens (O. P.) 83–84, 86–88
Spivey, H. J. 46, 48
Stone, Barton Warren (Barton W.) 2–3, 5, 12, 19
Wallace, N. B. 36, 51–52, 55, 60–62, 64–68, 74–76
Weatherford, A. J. 4, 9–10, 44–45, 57, 61
Weatherford, T. C. 50
Weatherford, Thomas L. 31–34, 36, 41, 43, 46–53, 55–57, 64–70, 74–76, 78–80, 95–97, 101–102

Also by C. Wayne Kilpatrick

An Early History of the Mars Hill Church of Christ: With a Collection of Memories by Members of the Congregation (2024)

J. R. Bradley: A Forgotten Larimore Boy (2019)

John Chisholm Church History Series

including

A Little Band of Disciples: The Beginnings of Churches of Christ in Madison County, Alabama

A Faithful Band of Workers: The Beginnings of Churches of Christ in Jackson County, Alabama

A Noble Band of Worshipers: The Beginnings of Churches of Christ Lauderdale County, Alabama

A Small Band of Brethren: The Beginnings of Churches of Christ in Limestone County, Alabama

HERITAGE
CHRISTIAN UNIVERSITY
PRESS

CYPRESS

To see the full catalog of Heritage Christian University Press and its imprint, Cypress Publications, visit www.hcupress.edu

Milton Keynes UK
Ingram Content Group UK Ltd.
UKHW040255291024
450401UK00006B/59